DENIAL
OF JUSTICE

DENIAL

OF JUSTICE

Criminal Process in the United States

Lloyd L. Weinreb

THE FREE PRESS
A Division of Macmillan Publishing Co., Inc.
NEW YORK

Collier Macmillan Publishers
LONDON

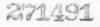

The Free Press
A Division of Macmillan Publishing Co., Inc.
866 Third Avenue, New York, N.Y. 10022

Collier Macmillan Canada, Ltd.

Library of Congress Catalog Card Number: 76–27222

Printed in the United States of America

printing number
1 2 3 4 5 6 7 8 9 10

Library of Congress Cataloging in Publication Data

Weinreb, Lloyd L
    Denial of justice.

    Includes bibliographical references and index.
    1.   Criminal procedure--United States.
2.   Law enforcement--United States.   I.   Title.
KF9619.W34   345'.73'05   76-27222
ISBN 0-02-934900-1

CONTENTS

PREFACE

Criminal process is no longer the exclusive property of the specialist. More than most legal topics, the investigation of crimes and prosecution of criminals interest the public generally. Our well-being, especially in cities where most of us now live, depends on the effectiveness of the response to crime and disorder. And the inherent drama of crime and punishment absorbs nearly everyone. Most people think they could describe a criminal trial more accurately than they could a civil trial or any of the other noncriminal proceedings that may have a large impact on their lives.

Since around 1960, not only the dramatic and the lurid crime stories have been news. A series of controversial decisions of the Supreme Court made momentary celebrities of people like Dollree Mapp and Danny Escobedo and directed public attention to technical matters of constitutional principle, legal doctrine, and rules of procedure that are lawyers' stock in trade. Newspaper readers became familiar with terms like "exclusionary rules," "Miranda warnings," and "plea bargaining" that were commonplace shorthand expressions for complicated issues.

For someone like myself, who is interested professionally

in criminal process, it has not always been easy to tell whether all these news stories really are the first or second leaders on page one or just appear to be because I am looking for them. It is sometimes startling to discover how little of one's professional concerns and activities are part of common experience. Still, there is little doubt that criminal process now holds an unusually large share of our attention. Whether this interest is part of an awakened awareness of the urban poor who are those most often arrested and prosecuted, or is due to a heightened and more widespread fear of crime is not evident; probably it is both.

The few pages of "black-letter law" that once sufficed to state the constitutional principles have been amplified by a mountainous outpouring of cases and commentary. Virtually all of the currently applicable law has its main exposition in opinions of the Supreme Court written since 1960. Even so, we need to know the dates of the opinions, because what was the rule in 1967 very likely is no longer precisely the rule now. In this area, as in others, developments have been swift, albeit not always consistent.

The source of this book was an increasing conviction that despite the furor that swirled around the Supreme Court's opinions, the Court's answers to the critical issues did not matter very much, because the wrong questions were being asked. Repeatedly, the dilemmas that we could not solve appeared to be the product of our own not inevitable assumptions, which we were unwilling (or unable) to re-examine. That conviction has been strengthened by a sense, which I share with many professional and lay persons alike, that for all the law that has been made and remade and unmade, the criminal process has changed little. The "revolution in criminal procedure" that people like to talk about seems to have been more like just spinning our wheels.

This book is about the criminal process in operation: not

the rules of law so much as who actually does what and how, and what the consequences are. My primary purpose is to explain and criticize our present practice and, above all, to demonstrate that its failings are not isolable, incidental features of a generally sound process but are its most characteristic features and intrinsic. Thus, for example, the forceful encounter between the police and an arrested person at the station house, which infects all the evidence that the police obtain there, is not a circumstance that rules will eliminate; it is *the* method of criminal investigation. (One of the most disturbing symptoms of our present situation is the existence of two distinct bodies of literature directed at the police and covering the same aspect of their work: the legal literature, written primarily by the courts, which tells the police how to do their work, and the literature of "police science," which tells them how to get their work done. Both bodies of literature are vast and take scarcely any account of the other except to disapprove or dismiss it.) Delays of anywhere from three months to a year between an arrest and final judgment are not the occasional happenstance of fallible human institutions; they are routine and dictated by the normal operation of the process. Plea bargaining is not a departure from the usual pattern but a fullfillment of it; it is the trial that indicates a breakdown. The use of the courtroom as an arena for pyrotechnics, where manipulative ability is prized and tactics and strategy determine professional conduct, is not an abuse of the lawyers' prerogative; within our adversary system, that is what is supposed to happen at trial.

Most of the objections to our criminal process that I have made in this book have been made before. Usually, however, they are considered separately, in the context of an assumption that our process basically is sound; and the proposed solution is some procedural change in keeping with the structure generally. If the process is examined as a whole, the comforting belief that "bad as it is, there is nothing better" is no longer convincing, and a change of procedure here and there appears, as it is, beside the point. To carry out our purposes, we need an entirely different process, which rests on different premises and relies on different institutional arrangements.

The model of an alternative criminal process presented in the concluding chapter depends on the arguments in the chapters that precede it. For the most part, I have simply followed the implications of objections to our criminal process to their reasonable conclusions, without, however, assuming in advance that the conclusions must be applied within the existing framework. Central to the model is the establishment of the office of an investigating magistracy, which would combine some of the functions now performed variously by the police, the prosecutor, defense counsel, and the court. "Continental" criminal procedure provided a direction for my thinking; in particular, the opportunity several years ago to observe closely all aspects of French criminal process helped me to visualize possibilities unlike those with which I was familiar. The reason for adopting a model like the one I have outlined, however, is not that something similar has worked acceptably elsewhere, but that that is where our own principles and experience lead.

While the adoption of a "magisterial" criminal process would require very large changes indeed, many small changes that have already been made point in that direction. Increased use of some sort of judicial proceeding to initiate a prosecution and even occasionally to investigate is suggestive, although it is mostly confined by the form of a preliminary examination or the grand jury. Freer pretrial discovery and experiments with pretrial conferences and omnibus proceedings undermine the habit of separate "cases" prepared in secret and isolation from one another. Stricter review of the performance of the prosecutor and defense counsel and greater willingness to invalidate a conviction if the performance of either fell short lead to a measure of objective control of the conduct of a trial and lessened reliance on the lawyers' wholly independent decisions. In my more hopeful moments, therefore, I think of my proposals as both prescriptive and predictive.

Many friends and colleagues helped me to write this book. Robert M. Fogelson gave me the benefit of his knowledge and understanding of the police as a social institution in this country. R. Kent Greenawalt helped me to sharpen my conclusions about many problems of criminal procedure, including particularly the privilege against self-incrimination. Both of them and Richard D. Parker read the manuscript and made fruitful substantive and editorial suggestions. Thomas O. Sargentich was a valuable research and editorial assistant during the final stages of preparation of the manuscript. I am glad to record here my thanks to these people and others, whose assistance and advice were so willingly given.

L.L.W.

DENIAL
OF JUSTICE

1

CRIMINAL PROCESS

Criminal process is one of the necessities of life in community, not its reward. At its best, even when we are convinced that justice has been done, condemnation of a criminal is not a happy event. We should not be surprised if our methods satisfy no one fully. What we should expect, just because criminal justice is such a disagreeable business, is the most constant effort, within understandable limitations of resources, energy, and human good will, to do the best we can. No amount of attention to the means will resolve debate about the ends of criminal justice; doubt and disagreement about what conduct should be criminal and how it should be punished will remain. We can be certain, however, that if we do not attend closely to the means, the most nobly conceived ends will be futile.

The function of criminal process is to determine criminal guilt with a view toward imposing a penalty. If it provides a civic education for some people (which is doubtful) or a public entertainment, so much the better; but these are not its function, any more than it is the function of the judicial system to provide comfortable berths for the friends of successful politicians, as it does. Nor is it the function of criminal process itself to punish or rehabilitate criminals or deter the commission of crime, although there too, it may be, so much the better if it does. Criminal process is not a means to redistribute income, or encourage patriotism, or promote individual expression, except incidentally.

The main body of this book explains how criminal process works most of the time and how it fails. It usually consists of a brief police investigation followed long afterwards by a judgment based either on a hasty negotiation between the defendant's lawyer and the prosecutor or, much less often, on a trial in which guilt is a consequence of a win or a loss. The police usually investigate no further than their initial response to the crime; they are interested in clearing cases, with little attention to the subsequent needs of a criminal prosecution. The officials who are responsible for the determination of guilt rely on the findings of the police and seldom conduct any considerable investigation of their own. Prosecution means mainly the passage of time, during which little happens to increase our confidence in the outcome. When a sentence finally is imposed, its separation from the crime by time and the circumstances of the prosecution deprive it of significance as punishment.

Scarcely anyone believes that this process is a good one, although the main grounds of objection vary. Judgments of guilt are reached haphazardly and aimlessly, without either the deliberation or the urgency that they merit. Both in substance and appearance, they lack the qualities of rationality and consistency. For no reason other than the inadequacy of the process, persons who have committed serious crimes are not convicted at all or are convicted of a minor offense having no relation to what they did. Standards of individual dignity and liberty that we regard as fundamental are pointlessly violated. It has been our habit to acclaim our noble pretensions at the same time that we lament the failures in practice. The pretensions sound increasingly empty and unconvincing; and our actual expectations fall far beneath them.

Stripped of inconsequential formalities and the rhetoric with which we surround them, many of our practices manifestly make no sense. The methods of criminal investigation ought to produce an accurate account of a crime, with the least intrusion on people's lives. We cannot always meet both of those objectives as well as we should like; the fuller achievement of one may demand some sacrifice of the other. Often, however, we might come closer to both than we do. Investigative techniques would be more reliable if they were not tied to a forceful capture by the police, as many of them are now; and they would be less intrusive. For example, if our intention is that a lineup for identification of a suspect be as reliable, as respectful of his dignity, and as little nuisance for him or anyone else as we can make it, there are better ways to do it than to conduct a hasty lineup at the police station in the wake of his arrest.

A criminal prosecution ought to provide promptly a full consideration of all the facts relevant to the defendant's guilt and a convincing record to support the imposition of punishment. We should not, then, begin by hiding from the defense the evidence that the police gather at the scene of the crime until it has been fixed as part of the government's case. We should not allow the prosecutor and defense counsel to arrange a plea of guilty with scarcely any attention to the precise facts, or allow the defendant to plead guilty to a crime which he says he did not commit or which is logically impossible.[3] We should not allow the two lawyers to shape every aspect of a trial, including even the selection of the jury, according to their private calculations of what will advance their respective positions. If punishment is to be a deterrent to crime, it should not be postponed for months, easily stretching out to a year or more, while nothing happens.

It is a dangerous self-deception to attribute the deficiencies of criminal process simply to lack of resources or inevitable human failings, as we commonly do. The social resources now committed to it are not used nearly as productively as they might be; and we are not in any event likely to spend much more in the future. Public officials and professional people who are responsible for investigation and prosecution perform their duties ably. The irrational procedures that we employ are not irregularities of an otherwise sound process; they constitute the process itself. Were a person caught in the act of robbing another person prosecuted and convicted fairly and reliably within a day or two, it would be an aberration.

Because our criminal process fails to perform its function, criminal justice is denied. There is a link between guilt and penalty that distinguishes criminal justice from all other kinds of social imposition. Military service may last longer and be harder than imprisonment; but we understand the difference between performance of a duty, however onerous, and punishment. We take account of the understanding by our insistence that we not convict and punish an innocent person, even though the social cost of avoiding that mistake is sometimes very large.

We can reasonably claim that we have avoided convictions of persons who are incontestably not guilty, the "wrong man," as much as we practicably can. Appalling as such occurrences are, they are very rare and almost always attributable to a nonsystemic fault peculiar to the case, like malicious abuse of the process or a coincidence against which we cannot effectively guard. It is difficult to assert with confidence that a different process would reduce still more the small number of convictions that are wrong in that sense. One may be led to conclude, therefore, that at least so far as those who are convicted are concerned, our process is not unjust.

While the conviction and punishment of someone who is wholly innocent is the most plain and unequivocal denial of justice, we do not establish the justice of punishment simply by showing that someone has committed a crime. The words that we use to characterize most crimes, like "robbery," "murder," or "kidnapping," serve us both descriptively and prescriptively; they describe an event and prescribe a penalty. Focusing on their descriptive content, it is easy for us to say that if a man has in fact committed a robbery, he is guilty of that crime whatever may be true of anyone else. We slide easily from that statement to the quite different statement that if a man has in fact committed a robbery, the verdict against him should be "guilty of robbery," and he should be punished accordingly whatever may be true of anyone else. Although it may be socially useful and satisfying to convict him of robbery even though fifty other robbers are not similarly convicted, our failure to convict them is not immaterial to his claim that he is dealt with unjustly. The accuracy of his conviction as a prescription for punishment and the justice of the punishment that is imposed depend on what happens to other persons who commit similar acts.

Within a human community, we have to accept something less than certain, universal justice, of course. The issue is not that, but the maintenance of a criminal process that is visibly careless, pervasively and systematically, of the connection between guilt and punishment of those whom it convicts. It gives us no assurance that we have done as well as we can to provide that our judgments of guilt and the punishments we impose have the same basis and meaning in all cases. Often, without reason, we fail to convict in circumstances indistinguishable from those in which others are convicted.

It is not difficult to find implicit or express in many defenses of our procedures the attitude that their chief virtue is that they are so erratic. Given the awful conditions of our prisons and the doubtful social value of more imprisonment, one may look with relief at the very inefficiency of the criminal process, which, unevenly and uncertainly to be sure, keeps the rough engine of criminal law from grinding too hard. The society that proposes to utilize criminal process, however, cannot meet the charge that the process is unjust by pointing to claims of other, larger injustice that the society has rejected. We cannot use criminal process to enforce the law and at the same time defend it against claims of injustice by observing that it mitigates, arbitrarily and without principle, the injustice of the law it enforces. Our concern, after all, ought to be for those who are convicted and punished, who are not dealt with more justly because some other persons who might also have been punished are allowed to escape.

The demands that criminal process be effective and that it be just are not opposed. An effective process is not one that indiscriminately increases the number of convictions of the guilty at whatever sacrifice of other values, any more than a just process is one that indiscriminately decreases it. We cannot sustain our authority to punish on any ground, whether of social utility or of desert, while we exercise it with so little concern for the outcome. Whether one believes that criminal justice is finally no more than social engineering or that it is an effort to do justice in a larger sense, the requirements of rationality and fairness are the same.

There has been no lack of discussion about criminal process, which characteristically takes the form of a conflict between "law and order" and individual rights. Public figures call for the community to "get tough" with criminals or, on the other side, protest against what they regard as encroachments on our civil liberties. The judiciary has participated in the discussion at another, usually less strident level. In a brief period of about ten years, corresponding roughly to the sixties, the courts carried out what has frequently been described as a "revolution" in criminal procedure. Relying on clauses in the Bill of Rights, the Supreme Court imposed on both state and federal prosecutions a series of constitutional requirements which appeared to give the defendant large new rights.[2] Since 1970 there has been something of a "counter-revolution"; a different majority on the Court has qualified the doctrines so recently announced and emphasized the importance of convicting the guilty.[3] During both periods, dissenters on the Supreme Court (and lower courts) have made certain that decisions were reached with at least the appearance of thorough consideration.

Our understanding of the criminal process and confidence in it have not been increased. Far from resolving doubts, persistent controversy seems to have convinced most people that the important issues are beyond balanced resolution and are decided only by the play of political force. Too often, in the courts as much as elsewhere, what parades as a reasoned argument looks uncomfortably like a naked effort to gain as much as one can when the votes are there. The justices of the Supreme Court themselves have repeatedly accused one another of distorting the Court's previous opinions and manipulating doctrine to achieve a desired result. Evidence to support the accusations is abundant. At the height of the judicial "revolution," Congress enacted legislation purporting to overrule some of the Court's key constitutional rulings. The question whether Congress had the authority to do so has not been answered, and the statutes and decisions remain to contradict one another.[4]

It is a bootless enterprise to continue to debate legal principles without confronting the overriding reality that our methods of investigating and prosecuting crime are fundamentally unresponsive to our needs. The procedures to which we formally adhere treat a crime as a separate, striking event in which everyone might take an interest and a prosecution as a distinct act of justice. Nowadays, for most of us crimes are not discrete events so much as they are a condition of life; they compose a mass within which one crime is distinguished from another only by the people directly involved. Perforce, in the working model of criminal process results are measured statistically. The institutions on which we primarily rely to carry out the process—the police, the prosecutor's office, and the legal profession—perform their tasks as they can; but they are not organized or equipped to act as, according to our theory, they are supposed to do.

Even when we argue most earnestly about this or that legal principle, therefore, there is not much likelihood that any principle we finally adopt will be followed systematically in practice. The most important application of the Supreme Court's rulings about police behavior, for example, is the exclusion of evidence. If the police question a suspect abusively, his admissions of guilt in response to their questions may not be used against him. If they violate his constitutional protection against unlawful search and seizure, the prosecutor cannot use what the search turns up. These exclusionary rules are the subject of intense controversy. The police and their supporters insist that a criminal should not go free because the police have made a misstep. Civil libertarians exclaim just as loudly that the government should not profit from its own wrongdoing. The rules have had a striking impact in a small number of cases. But they have not affected the general behavior of the police or the likelihood of a conviction nearly as much as the furor over them suggests. They are significant within the theoretical framework of a prosecution as an individually important, coherent whole, to which each of its parts is responsive. But the police are not so concerned about prosecution, the judicial process is not so able to evaluate the behavior of the police, and exclusion of evidence does not so often determine whether there is a conviction as the premises of the rules require. If we are as serious as we profess to be about the constitutional rights that the exclusionary rules are supposed to protect, we need to find a better way to protect them.

Similarly, the pronouncement in 1963 that every defendant prosecuted for a felony is entitled to the aid of a lawyer was made with considerable fanfare. Legal counsel for all, the Supreme Court said, was essential to the "noble ideal" that "every defendant stands equal before the law."[5] For the next nine years, the Court, evidently troubled by the issue, refused to decide whether the same rule applies to minor crimes, misdemeanors, as well; and then said that it does if the penalty is imprisonment.[6] Despite the Court's pronouncements, the "noble ideal" is too obviously only that. The very dependence of our criminal process on the individual performances of the prosecutor and defense counsel that makes the appointment of counsel so critical ensures that whether or not defendants stand equal before the law, they fall unequally under its judgments. Equal justice would be far more likely if we recognized the excesses of the adversary system and eliminated them instead of pretending, contrary to what we all know, that the excesses do not matter so long as we formally assign a lawyer to people who cannot afford to pay for one.

In this book I have largely avoided controversies about constitutional principles. Instead of the usual emphasis on individual rights and official duties, I have emphasized how investigation and prosecution are actually performed and how they could be performed better. That approach indicates no disregard for the values which the Constitution protects. On the contrary, we shall realize those values more fully and certainly if we do not insist on giving them a meaning in theory that we are obliged to ignore in practice. More than we have recognized, conflicts within criminal process between efficient law enforcement and individual liberty are irreconcilable only if we take for granted the institutional and procedural framework in which they now arise.

The criminal process that is discussed in this book is followed in most prosecutions for a serious crime. While local practice varies from state to state and sometimes within a state, the variations are largely matters of form underneath which the substance is remarkably similar. In some respects the harshness of the process in big cities may be mitigated in rural areas where there is not the constant pressure of a "crime problem"; but its important features are rarely different. I have not paid attention to the vast number of minor offenses like public drunkenness, disorderly conduct, and petty shoplifting. Such crimes are disposed of summarily in truncated proceedings that are only a distorted shadow of what is described here, although as a wholly formal matter they are not so different. At the other extreme, an occasional case may follow a course different from what I have described. Those are exotic trees that should not affect our view of the forest.

In the concluding chapter, I have described in broad outline what a better process, suited to our purposes, might look like. While there is disagreement about almost every detail of criminal process, opposition to really substantial change is always clamorous. There is an overriding belief among lawyers and scholars and the public generally that our way of doing things is fundamentally right, especially in contrast with the way a prosecution is conducted elsewhere. When the basic structure is challenged, it is defended; and its faults and failings are dismissed as merely the tax that theory pays to practice. Having argued at length that our way of doing things is fundamentally wrong, I intend the outline of an alternative process as a response to the mistaken belief, against which Tocqueville warned, that confounds the familiar with the necessary. My object is not so much to offer a blueprint for specific changes, which should be the product of experiment and experience, but to provide a background against which our present practices can be displayed.

In many respects, the alternative resembles the process elsewhere that we pejoratively label the "continental" or "inquisitorial" system. The connotations of such labels betray our xenophobic prejudices. It is not, after all, immaterial that most of the countries of the world, many no less committed to liberty and justice than our own, rely on procedures so different from ours. At the same time, the proposals that I make are intended to respond to our own circumstances and not to compose an "ideal" process. Unless one starts (and finishes) with a view of man according to which his nature is not determined much at all by his surroundings, it is implausible that criminal process should be everywhere alike. The particular forms that it takes are much more reflective of a society's ground rules, its social and political philosophy and institutions, than is generally remarked. French *procédure pénale,* for example, is profoundly affected by the concept of *L'Etat,* the State, as an entity whose authority is not to be questioned (even when it is not precisely obeyed). While the proposals here are similar to French procedure in many respects, they would not work out in the same way in this country, where "the authority of the state" is not a reason for doing anything.

Most of us do not expect to become involved personally in the criminal process. Other matters raise issues of more immediate concern. Those who are professionally engaged in the process and are most conscious of its deficiencies have expectations and interests that are based on it, even though they may deplore it otherwise. General dissatisfaction with the criminal process is, however, very strong and cannot be traced to particular political attitudes. Lack of confidence in its methods and its results contributes to a sense of loss of liberty and order both. Too often, whether a person who has committed a crime finally is convicted or not, the aims of criminal law are needlessly frustrated. Within the course of criminal justice itself, justice is denied.

2

CRIMINAL INVESTIGATION

The investigation of crime in the United States is based on the premise that keeping the peace and investigating crime are parts of a single enterprise, the "war against crime," for which the police are responsible. Guided by that premise, the rules of law and public discussions about the law are concerned above all with the behavior of the police: what they can and cannot do in an encounter with someone who may be involved somehow in a crime. Critical issues are cast in terms of a contest between the authority of the police and the autonomy of private persons. Resolution of the issues generally takes the form of a balance between those contending forces which, perforce, comes down in favor of one or the other.

The main argument of this chapter, which is a major theme of the book, is that the assumption that peacekeeping and developing proof of a crime are inseparable is a bad one,

13

which no amount of legal refinements will improve very much. As keepers of the peace, the police often respond to crimes in circumstances that put the criminal's guilt beyond question. But the deliberate preparation of a case against the defendant is an aspect of a criminal prosecution, not crime prevention. If the war against crime is one enterprise, then to extend the metaphor, the police should not be fighting on both fronts at once. Their responsibility, for which they are uniquely qualified, is keeping the peace and maintaining the order of the community. The investigative function, except when it is an incidental consequence of peacekeeping, is one for which they are not qualified and which they perform badly. Their lack of qualification is not one that a change of the law will remedy, because the very qualities that equip them as peacekeepers are the ones that disqualify them for prosecutorial investigation.

Evidence that something is seriously wrong with our current approach is not lacking. The law does not make sense. Its fine distinctions elude understanding even in the quietude of a courtroom, to say nothing of the harried circumstances of a police patrol. Clauses of the Bill of Rights that protect basic liberties are freighted with epicycles that may fascinate analysts of a scholastic bent but no one else.[1] As for the police, to whom the rules are supposed to speak, they after all have a job to do. They do their job as they see it, with an eye cocked at the law but their minds—and their hearts—elsewhere. For all the rule making and remaking, the behavior of the police in a criminal situation has not changed very much in its essentials. We have grown uncomfortably familiar with the discontinuity between the rhetoric of the law and the practical realities of law enforcement. Purporting to affect what the police do, courts render their decisions confident that the police will manage.[2] The police, for their part, listen respectfully—and circulate mimeographed analyses of the latest judicial opinions—and then go to work.

While our dependence on the police has increased vastly in the last hundred years, paralleling the increasing complexity of urban life, the most important aspect of their work always has been that it is not confined to specific tasks. Their overriding duty is a general one: to maintain public order and restore the peace of the community when it is disturbed. They are expected to be alert to disturbances and to act on their own initiative to end them. For most people, they are also a residual social service. They are liable to be called in any emergency not within the duties of more precisely defined social agencies like the fire and sanitation departments: injuries and deaths, burst sewer pipes, cats in trees, children in locked bathrooms, family quarrels, barroom brawls. The occasions when the police are called vary among different economic and social neighborhoods; but the general principle is that the police are an undifferentiated source of help. When they are called, unless they can recommend a more appropriate agency, they are expected to respond. The police do not say, "Sorry, that's not our job."

Whatever we may criticize about their performance, the police are remarkably well equipped for these general functions. The essential characteristics of the police are determined by them. Men and equipment—cars, radios, stationhouses—are deployed to allow the police to perform all their regular assignments, including peacekeeping patrols, and still to respond swiftly whenever and wherever they are needed within their jurisdiction. Large items in the police budget are traceable directly to efforts to increase their readiness to respond: fleets of cruising police cars connected by a sophisticated communications system, "call boxes," strategically located sub-stations. The amount of time it takes the police to appear after they are summoned, what they call "response time," is regarded as a critical indicator of effectiveness by themselves and citizens alike.

The authority of the police conforms to these tasks and expectations. When they answer a summons to a private house, they may act by invitation and need no special authority. If an invitation is lacking, in a genuine emergency involving serious danger to persons or property their independent authority to enter, by force if they must, and take action to meet the danger is not disputed. Nor is their authority to issue directions and commands during a public disturbance seriously questioned. We do not doubt, for example, that the police can halt traffic or reroute pedestrians as the occasion requires.

How much of this kind of policing there should be and how it should be accomplished are matters of debate and sometimes bitter disputes. Particularly in the densely populated, rundown areas of a city, residents may believe that the police give them less protection than they are entitled to have. The peacekeeping operations of the police are restricted not only by the city's budget but also by the unpleasantness of too visible, too intrusive preventive patrolling. It is a persistent dilemma to provide the protection against disorder that people want without creating resentment of the police because of the methods they use to provide it. From their point of view, "walking tall," telling small streetcorner crowds to "break it up" and "move it along," and generally increasing awareness of their presence have the effect of preserving order. The people who feel the weight of such tactics view them as harassment, even if they also feel the need for protection.

However we resolve such problems, the connection between the peacekeeping function of the police and their capacities and authority is close and convincing. Whatever other functions they are assigned, wisely or not, and whatev-

we may want to prosecute him later, we need to know who he is; we need the usual indicia of identity like name and address that connect us from one time and place to another. It is possible that the officer could obtain such information on the spot, as he does when a driver is stopped for a traffic offense. But in the charged atmosphere of an arrest for a more serious crime, it would usually be too much to ask of an officer that he solicit information from the person he has just arrested or examine documents of identification then and there.

When the police reach the scene of a crime after the criminal is gone, if there is any likelihood that he may be found and prosecuted later the police have a duty to gather some information. Their immediate task is not to resolve doubts about what happened or even to gather all the information that might be relevant. We do not expect a police officer to have the skills of a lawyer or judge; nor do we expect him to conduct an inquest on the sidewalk. But as the only officials on the scene, the police have to gather enough information to preserve the possibility of a more thorough and precise investigation later. That includes identifying the victim and witnesses, securing physical evidence that might be altered or disappear,* and making notes of facts that may later be significant: weather conditions perhaps, someone's state of sobriety, and so forth.

Just as the immediate tasks of peacekeeping may serve functions necessary for a prosecution later, when the police gather information at the scene of a crime, that investigative function helps to restore order. One of the ways that police confronted by a disturbed victim and witnesses can take control without giving too many commands or displaying too

---

*The woman whose purse was snatched may rejoice at its recovery only to find to her dismay that the police and prosecutor impound it as evidence until the case is disposed of.

much force is to ask questions: "O.K., now, everyone take it easy. What happened? One at a time. ONE AT A TIME!" By asking questions they display public concern and call on people to calm down and reflect. If the criminal is gone, there is not much else that the police can do. (Suppose that the woman's assailant had made good his escape and the officer had said only, and accurately, "Well, I guess he's gone. May as well go buy a new pocketbook, ma'am.")

The investigation of most crimes does not go any further. A victim of one of the ordinary crimes against strangers, like a mugging or housebreaking, discovers to his surprise that after the police have looked around and asked some questions—"What was taken?" "What did the assailant look like?"—their work is about over. If there are obvious leads, they will be pursued; it may be practical to show witnesses photographs from a "mug file" or, much less frequently, to dust for fingerprints. Probably there are no leads. In a very small number of special cases, the police investigate intensively and persistently: murder, especially the killing of a policeman, sensational holdups, and some others. Aside from such exceptional cases, crimes are cleared because the victim or witnesses know the criminal and can identify him or because he is caught in the act or soon afterwards in circumstances that put his guilt beyond question.

Most often, therefore, what we think of as the investigative work of the police is not separate from the more general peacekeeping function or very different from what they do when they respond to the scene of a noncriminal disturbance. Situations that turn out to involve a crime often do not appear so from the start, or the reverse. Called to a private home or a bar to quiet a disturbance, or making a routine stop at the emergency ward of the city hospital on Saturday night, police may find a person badly wounded with no immediate indication whether he is the victim of a crime or a criminal or whether any crime was committed at all.

We cannot change the pattern of police behavior in such situations without affecting their primary responsibility as peacekeepers. They perform their tasks, asking questions and so forth, at the scene of the crime not because these are done better there than in the calmer atmosphere of a courtroom or a hospital, but because performance "on location" is part of the definition of the tasks. They do not make their judgments swiftly because they are more likely to be accurate that way, but because there is no time for deliberation and consultation. The police have force at their disposal and are ready to use it not because force is a good thing, but because the circumstances are such that what we want done may require it, and we are willing to accept that. Were we to decide for any reason that the police should behave differently, instead of prescribing rules to modify their behavior the sensible course would be not to provide the costly resources on which their capacity to act with mobility, speed, and force depend.

Criminal investigation was not identified originally as a separate or special responsibility of urban police departments. In the nineteenth century, the local constabulary retained many of the characteristics of their original, the town watchman. Their duty was in a small way to keep the peace and public order; and they performed whatever other related or unrelated functions were assigned to them. On rare occasions, when an unsolved crime was spectacular enough to disturb public order, they might become involved in investigative work. In some cities police undertook not so much to solve crimes or capture criminals as to regulate crime so that it did not become a disturbance; "regulation" might include acting as receiver of stolen goods, which were returned to their owners not in the line of duty but for a reward. Like most services, the prevention and detection of crime were left mainly to private enterprise. Railroads, mining companies, and other large businesses employed their own police forces to protect their property. Individuals who could afford it hired private detectives from agencies like Pinkerton.

After the turn of the century, when immigration had swollen the number of the urban poor, crime became a social problem for which a social solution was needed. The assignment fell naturally to the police, who were jacks-of-all-trades anyway. So far as the solution might be patrol of the streets and a swift response, the assignment to them made sense; it was after all precisely the nature of their work to be on the street and keep order when there was trouble.

The police have assiduously cultivated their image as "crimefighters" as part of a campaign for professional respectability. Before World War I, their desire for the status of professionals was encouraged by the Progressive political movement, which used professionalism as a weapon against ward politics. Adoption of a military analogy for the police, with its attendant vocabulary, dress, and manner; persistent emphasis on crime statistics; newspaper coverage of the sensational—all served that image. Above all, the police insisted that criminal investigation was highly technical work, a "science," which required skill and training and produced spectacular results. The importance of investigative technique was emphasized in 1908 when the Department of Justice opened a small Bureau of Investigation. John Edgar Hoover, who became Director of the Bureau in 1924, made superior training and ability its trademark; and by 1935, when it was renamed the Federal Bureau of

Investigation, its reputation as a professionally trained and equipped investigative force had been established.

To a considerable extent, the police have accomplished their aim. Their public image is suggested by the movies and television, where the Keystone cop, an incompetent, well-meaning buffoon, has been replaced by Joe Friday and Kojak, single-minded, earnest investigators of crime. The police have at least as strong a professional identity as firemen, with whom they used to be unfavorably compared; and they have achieved equality or primacy in status and rewards among the non-white-collar public services. In the last two decades, educational and other characteristically professional requirements for entry into police work have proliferated, along with special university programs in criminal justice and "police science."

While crime occupies the attention of the police much more than before, they are still a general service force. Even if routine, nonemergency duties like traffic control are left aside, most encounters between the police and the public do not involve a crime.* Many of the most common police incidents, like family assaults and minor street disturbances, could be treated as crimes but seldom are. Because the police are now regarded as crimefighters, however, actions that are readily understood as peacekeeping measures are treated as if their purpose were exclusively to initiate a criminal prosecution. And at the same time the police have acquired a distinct set of functions connected not with peacekeeping, but with the preparation of a case for prosecution. We have neither trained nor equipped them for this work nor given them proper authority to carry it out; and they are generally not competent to do it.

*The assignment of traffic control to the police is a reflection of their position as jacks-of-all-trades. There is not an inevitable connection

ARREST

The slender bond which holds the inconsistent, divergent responsibilities of the police together is the law of arrest. Because of the insistent association of the police with crime we may now think of an arrest as their most characteristic act. For the most part, however, it is not based on any special authority. Under the old English and American law and still today in most states, anyone has authority to arrest someone whom he sees committing a crime. Nowadays, of course, few people exercise that authority except the police, to whom we have collectively assigned our responsibility as citizens. The law defines an arrest as taking a person into custody in order to hold him to answer for an offense. Police officers (or under the common law anyone else) may arrest someone if they have "probable cause" to believe that he has committed a crime. They have probable cause if the "'facts and circumstances within [the arresting officers'] knowledge and of which they had reasonably trustworthy information [are] sufficient in themselves to warrant a man of reasonable caution in the belief that' an offense has been or is being committed."[3] There are some finer points about authority to arrest, but they can fairly be described as details. For practical purposes, the requirement of probable cause is what counts.

The courts, the Supreme Court leading the way, have debated long and hard—and tediously—about the precise kind and quantum of evidence that adds up to probable

---

between that and their other assignments, as the increasing use of meter readers and other paraprofessionals for routine traffic duty makes clear. It is not irrelevant either to the ability of the FBI as genuine criminal investigators or to their image as professionals that they have never been regarded as general peacekeepers or simply jacks-of-all-trades.

cause. They have measured the precise weight to be given an unnamed informer's tip, uncorroborated hearsay, inferences from circumstantial evidence, and so forth. Such analysis resembles considerably the efforts of medieval legalists to label and measure every kind of evidence and develop a mathematical system of "proof"; and it is about as persuasive. One may see in such hyper-rationalization of the standard for an arrest uneasy recognition that arrests are often made when they are functionally pointless.

On its face, an arrest is a custodial measure taken because it is believed that the person has probably committed a crime and should be held for trial. The fact that no one except the police ordinarily makes an arrest is explained by our reliance on them generally for the prevention of crime and their presence at the scene of crimes. Accordingly, when the police arrest someone, they are simply initiating custody, with the immediate objective of surrendering him to the authorities responsible for prosecution. But in fact most persons who are arrested are not prosecuted, and of those who are prosecuted most are not held for trial, but are released soon after their arrest. The treatment of arrest as if it were a custodial measure dependent only on the existence of probable cause distorts what the police do. When they have peacekeeping functions to perform, it imposes a requirement which, if it were taken seriously, would often prevent them from doing what we want done; and it distracts our attention from the question of how we want it done. On the other hand, so long as the requirement of probable cause is met, the police have been allowed additional authority to conduct prosecutorial investigation unrelated to the supposed function of an arrest.

When the police stop a person's movement on the street or detain him momentarily to carry out their peacekeeping functions, we do not ordinarily regard the interference as an arrest if it is brief and ends on the street. A police officer directing traffic does not "arrest" drivers in the lanes he stops. Nor does an officer who commands people to "keep back" from a fire "arrest" them all, even though he may in some sense have interfered with their liberty. We do not ordinarily describe it as a mass arrest when an officer commands everyone at the scene of a crime to "stay put." In the same way, apprehension of a person leaving the scene of a crime may be justified as a peacekeeping measure without regard to the likelihood of a subsequent prosecution. We do not expect the police officer coming to the aid of the woman who has just been mugged to deliberate whether he has probable cause to believe the woman before he goes after her apparent assailant; it may turn out that she is drunk or has pointed to the wrong man, or that the man is her husband who knocked her down in lawful self-defense after she attacked him with her purse. In a situation of that kind, as in situations which do not involve an apparent crime, if the restraint is brief and ends without more, we generally treat it as a peacekeeping measure and do not regard it as an arrest. But if it turns out that a crime has (apparently) been committed and the man is not released then and there, the restraint is treated exclusively as an arrest to which the requirement of probable cause applies. The peacekeeping function is ignored and the man's apprehension and restraint are treated from the beginning as if the police officer's sole purpose had been to take him into custody.

The distortion that results is illustrated by a case in the District of Columbia in 1969. Just after midnight several men attacked Grady Johnson and Henry Ussery on the sidewalk. A wallet, a watch, and some money were taken from Johnson, and a watch and penknife from Ussery. Police officers arrived within a few minutes. A small crowd had gathered. Bruised and bleeding about his face, Ussery pointed to one of the men in the crowd, a stranger to him, and told the police that the man was one of those who had robbed him. Ussery was excited and admitted that he had been drinking; but he said he was sure of the identification.[4] What should the police officer have done if at that point the man to whom Ussery pointed had started to walk away? It seems doubtful at best that there was probable cause to believe the man was one of the robbers, not least because we should not expect him to have stayed around to watch if he were. Does it matter? Do we want the police to ponder whether there is probable cause before they do anything? To what purpose?

In the actual case, a police officer told the unidentified man that Ussery had accused him. The man denied the accusation and said that he was out for a walk and had just come on the scene. What then? The police officer searched the man and found the watches and the penknife. It is perhaps debatable whether it was proper to search the man's pockets before any other check was made, although it is hard to believe that at least his detention was not an appropriate measure to restore order. But it wholly misconceives the situation to assert that the only question is whether the police had probable cause to arrest the man before he was searched, on the basis of Ussery's doubtful identification.* To train and equip and direct the officer to keep the peace and at the same time tell him that probable cause is all that counts is to give contradictory messages, one of which he has to ignore. As the case turned out, the courts made a questionable finding that there was probable cause in order

---

*Under existing law, the arrest could not be justified by what the search turned up because the only basis for the search was a precedent lawful arrest.

to sustain a police action that most of us would consider proper for entirely different reasons, whether there was probable cause or not.

Another case, which reached the Supreme Court, illustrates how our fixed focus on probable cause may encourage police conduct that none of us should approve. Two detectives saw Jose Rios enter a taxicab in an area of Los Angeles known for "narcotics activity." They did not know him but were suspicious for some reason and followed him in an unmarked car for about two miles. The taxicab stopped for a red light. "The two officers alighted from their car and approached on foot to opposite sides of the cab. One of the officers identified himself as a policeman. In the next minute there occurred a rapid succession of events. The cab door was opened; the petitioner dropped a recognizable package of narcotics to the floor of the vehicle; one of the officers grabbed the petitioner as he alighted from the cab; the other officer retrieved the package; and the first officer drew his revolver."[5]

Rios was prosecuted for unlawful possession of narcotics. In their original arrest report, the officers had said that Rios dropped the package after one of them had opened the door of the taxi. At the trial, months after the arrest, the officer who opened the door testified that Rios had dropped the package first. After passing through the federal appellate court, the case was decided by the Supreme Court. The Court reasoned that the officers did not have probable cause for an arrest before they saw the package but did after they saw it, since it was readily identifiable as containing narcotics and the possession of narcotics is ordinarily unlawful. Therefore, the Court concluded, it was necessary to determine precisely when in the "rapid succession of events" the arrest occurred. The case was sent back to the trial court. Four years after the arrest, the judge made findings about the sequence of events. He found that Rios was not arrested until he dropped the package in plain view of the officers. The conviction was therefore affirmed.

We are entitled to be skeptical about the ability of the trial judge to make a serious factual determination about so small a detail in a brief, sudden encounter, so long after the event.* That aside, it is remarkable that the detail should have such significance. So far as the record in the Supreme Court shows, no other issue was raised about the conduct of the police. Was it good work to follow the taxi? Should two police officers in plain clothes, with no more reason than those officers had, approach a taxi from both sides at a street intersection at night? What could they and should they have done if Rios had not fortuitously dropped narcotics in plain view at just the right moment? After the events which so occupied the courts, Rios got out of the cab. He tried to run away. One of the policemen shot him in the back and apprehended him. Was that good police work?

From any point of view, including their own, the detectives should not have behaved as they did. The likelihood that someone, not necessarily the man they intended to accost, would be hurt was too great. Their unelaborated suspicion did not justify the danger to themselves or others or the disturbance of the peace that resulted. Furthermore, the startling outcome of the event should not obscure the fact that their initial action, resting on as slight a basis as they had, was needless harassment. The courts' unnerving emphasis on probable cause to take Rios into custody excluded inquiry into any of those issues.

---

*According to the judge's own findings, the whole encounter lasted "about one minute." United States v. Rios, 192 F. Supp. 888, 890 (S.D. Cal. 1961).

The custodial justification for an arrest generally has as little to do with its consequences as it does with the reasons that precipitate it. Theoretically, once the police have taken a person into custody, their only duty is to bring him promptly before a magistrate. There is no reason to detain him at the police station any longer than is necessary to locate a magistrate, or to take him to the station at all if a magistrate is available immediately. In practice, however, the police carry out an extensive range of procedures at the police station as a matter of course; release of the arrested person to judicial authority is deliberately postponed until they are completed. The procedures fall into two groups: booking and prosecutorial investigation.

Booking. When he arrives at the police station, an arrested person is routinely "booked."* The fact of his arrest, some personal data, his fingerprints, and his photograph are made part of a permanent record. Booking is not onerous; it is not worse than all kinds of routine procedures that are part of ordinary life. A police officer assigned to clerical duty asks for information which is neither very private nor very unusual and records it on a standard form: identifying data, like name, address, and age; physical data, like hair and eye color; data of public record, like place of birth and military experience; and a few other facts like place of work and family relationships. Fingerprinting and photographing are carried out swiftly and without unpleasantness unless the person resists. Booking is accepted as a standard arrest practice, and few people object. If someone does object, the police are not likely to make a great deal of it; "Be a wiseguy if you want" is as likely a response as any.

*The word probably derives from the common practice of entering the name and some other brief data about the arrest in a large

Since we do readily comply with comparable procedures in so many contexts, it is difficult to argue that booking
at the police station is a violation of individual rights. It is,
however, generally quite useless. The practice of booking
developed after 1920 when the movement for professionalism had overtaken police departments; the keeping of
records was regarded as one of the marks of the professional.
It was widely declared that the accumulation of information
about persons who were arrested would reduce crime.[6] The
FBI, which conducts a vast criminal statistics operation,
encourages and helps local police to do likewise. It has
developed an elaborate uniform reporting system and provides the standard forms on which information and fingerprints are recorded. Most important, it maintains a central
depository for arrest records from all sources; copies of the
records are transmitted to it and disseminated in response to
inquiries from local police departments and other official
agencies.*

Led by the FBI and spurred by the bureaucratic habit of

---

ledger-type book as soon as the person is brought in. That entry, which
is not what we now think of as booking, is meant to serve the purpose of
keeping track of persons brought to the station, lest they "disappear"
there for a long period. It is sadly characteristic of our high principles
and low practices that we do not carry out that purpose by requiring the
police to allow an arrested person immediately to call someone in his
family or a friend or to do so for him; nor do we require, as in some
countries, that the station record of arrests be examined regularly by a
judicial official having the responsibility to supervise detention.

*The FBI's current objective, which is near achievement, is an
Automated Identification Division System, which "will eventually provide for automatic fingerprint searching, computerized name searching
of the criminal name indices, computer storage and retrieval of arrest
record data, and the capability to gather criminal statistics and system
performance data." Conrad S. Banner and Robert M. Stock, "The FBI's
Approach to Automatic Fingerprint Identification," *FBI Law Enforcement
Bulletin,* February 1975, p. 26.

accumulating whatever information is easily accumulated, police departments have made the collection of data from arrested persons a large enterprise. The permanent recording of criminal arrests, most of which are not followed by a conviction or even a trial, has become a serious source of opposition to the police; opposition increases as the records become more comprehensive and the means of retrieving and disseminating them more efficient. While the police claim that their only interest in the records is their use in investigative work, the records are rarely useful for that purpose to the police or anyone else. The main use of arrest records is said to be the identification of a person arrested in one jurisdiction as someone wanted for a crime elsewhere. Occasionally, such an identification has significance beyond the mere fact itself; very rarely indeed, an identification may contribute to clearing a crime. But aside from the satisfaction it gives the police themselves to learn that an arrested person has been arrested before, the concrete value of such identifications in terms of convictions obtained or even crimes cleared has been greatly exaggerated.* The money spent to prepare and maintain the files could be used more effectively elsewhere in the police budget.

Fingerprinting as a standard postarrest procedure is equally hard to justify. Under the direction of the FBI, it has become an enormous and expensive operation, which is part of the Bureau's general program of obtaining as many fingerprints as possible from as many sources as possible.†

---

*The FBI obscures the question of utility by answering it with statistics showing how many identifications were made, which number in the millons. That answer confuses the question "How much did you accomplish?" with the quite different question "How much work did you do?"

†The FBI currently employs full-time more than 3,300 employees in its fingerprint operation, for which it requested an appropriation of $51,095,000 in the 1977 fiscal year.

Despite extravagant claims about its utility and a rare spectacular case, fingerprint records are not often valuable in criminal investigation. They are useful only to connect a person with an event in his past when he was fingerprinted. If fingerprints are recovered at the scene of a crime, which happens infrequently, prior fingerprint records are useful only to identify someone who is not otherwise suspected or whose fingerprints cannot otherwise be obtained. Impressive as the technology of fingerprinting is, we should not confuse the certainty of its findings when it is useful with general usefulness. The development and dissemination of fingerprinting technique is one of the FBI's achievements of which it is most proud. But particularly in view of its staggering cost, there are probably better ways to prevent crimes.*

The improper use of arrest records, on the other hand, is extensive. An arrest record may be regarded as relevant in a wide variety of contexts involving employment, education, public office, military service, credit, and so forth. Even if the official record itself is not disseminated beyond specific public agencies, which is not always the case, the maintenance of arrest records has encouraged private as well as

---

In the 1930's there was a widespread movement for universal fingerprinting on a voluntary or compulsory basis. The movement was finally defeated, partly by a campaign of the American Civil Liberties Union, which published a pamphlet called "Thumbs Down!" in 1938. Although universal compulsory fingerprinting has not been adopted, increasingly fingerprinting is required as the condition of some occupation or activity or is an incident of something like military service. The FBI usually receives copies of fingerprints made for these other purposes.

*In fact, the FBI did not originally make as much of the criminal uses of fingerprinting as it did of its civil uses, to aid in the identification of accident victims and so forth. Even now, there are fingerprints of roughly twice as many persons in the civil files as there are in the criminal files.

public agencies to give an arrest more significance than it should have. If we have confidence in the police at all, the fact that a person has been arrested is an indication of guilt. But it is the arresting officer's unverified belief, not the fact of the arrest, that is significant. Without the record of the event, we should not give so much weight to his bare belief without inquiring whether it proved to be accurate. If records of past criminal behavior are worth having for any purpose, they can be prepared at a later stage of the criminal process—when the person is formally accused of a crime or is convicted— with greater likelihood that they will reflect accurately what we want to know.*

Prosecutorial Investigation. The other set of procedures that has been tacked onto an arrest is closer to genuine investigative work. An arrested person is searched more thoroughly at the police station than he was at the place of the arrest; the search includes an examination of his clothing and belongings for evidence of any crime (like possession of drugs). If there is any reason to do so, he is placed in a lineup, where he may be required to make gestures, put on or take off clothing, speak words, or simply be viewed by witnesses. Some police stations routinely conduct a daily parade before the detectives of all arrested persons who were held overnight to see whether any of them fit descriptions in uncleared cases. A person may be required to give a

---

*Believing that such information is useful or at any rate that it is professional to have it, the police cannot be faulted for collecting it themselves rather than relying on the courts or prisons to do it at a later stage in the process; they have had little confidence in the ability of those institutions to accomplish what they think needs to be done.

Arrest records probably also have some psychological importance for the police. They give an arrest permanence and importance by transmuting the event into an object. Since for the police the arrest fulfills their independent responsibility in a criminal case, the transmutation is not a small thing.

sample of bodily substances like hair, fingernails, or blood. Finally, the police may question a person at length about the crime for which he was arrested or any other crime. Whether any or all of these procedures are carried out lies entirely within the discretion of the police. Provided only that the arrest is lawful, the procedures can be conducted without prior judicial approval, without any supervision, and without any showing then or later that they were reasonably necessary to any proper official function. Ordinarily, the desire of the police not to make needless work for themselves is our only assurance that they do not pointlessly invade people's privacy.

Search and questioning of suspects are practices which, within the constitutional framework, we are prepared to allow in appropriate circumstances.[7] Similarly, the Supreme Court has declared on the basis of long historical practice that identification and body-sampling techniques do not violate the privilege against self-incrimination.[8] So long as the person cooperates, none of them need involve violence or physical abuse. Nor is there doubt that such methods may provide substantial and reliable evidence of guilt. The question that needs to be asked is not whether they should ever be allowed or whether, like booking, they may not be largely useless. Rather, the question is why they should be authorized automatically after an arrest. The police have no general authority to require participation in procedures of this kind. We are not obliged to submit to a search or a lineup or questioning just because the police want us to. Not even the toughest advocates of "law and order" have suggested that the police be given so much power to intrude on our ordinary right to be let alone.

The concrete explanation for the connection between an arrest and the investigative practices that follow it is simply that the police have the responsibility for routine criminal investigation and do not have the authority to perform it otherwise. Whether or not they have probable cause to arrest someone, of course, there is no reason why the police cannot ask him to cooperate with them voluntarily, with less annoyance to everyone than an arrest would entail. And on a few occasions, the police have sought judicial authorization to conduct a lineup independently of an arrest. But conceiving themselves as crime fighters and working mostly in circumstances that do not accommodate polite requests or a judicial authorization, they have seldom resorted to either of those approaches.

On any more principled basis, there is no explanation for this aspect of police work. The argument that some courts have made that a person who has been arrested has no reason left to oppose all that may follow is simply false.[9] There is no reason why it *ought* to be true; and we know from experience how badly it describes the actual attitude of people who are arrested. On the other hand, we need not assume that if some investigative technique is appropriate, the only way to perform it is to arrest the person involved. We do not ordinarily "bring a man in" so that he may perform his obligations to the community. Even within the criminal process, most of the time defendants and witnesses are expected to perform their obligations in response to a notice, not by being removed forcibly to the place of performance. In a broad range of situations, people generally do what is required: tax returns are filed, traffic tickets paid, defendants and reluctant witnesses appear for trial, convicted defendants appear for sentencing and execution of sentence. So far as we have any experience to go on, it suggests that persons would respond often enough to make issuance of a summons preferable to an arrest. As in other circumstances, were a summons to appear for investigation not honored, the alternative of force would be available; but as a rule in our society, we do not resort to force first.

There are, furthermore, functional objections to our

dependence on a prior arrest for investigative purposes. In rare cases, like a blood test for alcohol content, a test has to be performed quickly lest an incriminating substance disappear; when the arrest was unforeseen, it may be necessary for the police to act then and there. More often, the haste with which the police act in the brief period they are allowed after an arrest undermines the utility of what they do. If there are witnesses to a crime, a reliable lineup may be the best means to confirm or refute suspicion of guilt. The circumstances at the police station following an arrest, however, usually do not afford much opportunity for a carefully controlled lineup; almost inevitably, a witness's identification raises suspicion of suggestiveness or prejudice if not indeed pressure on the witness. Dependence on an arrest may also have the consequence that an investigative measure that is most reasonable in the circumstances is not taken. For example, having witnesses to a crime but lacking probable cause for an arrest, the police are reduced to doubtful expedients like showing the witnesses photographs of the suspects or pointing the suspects out to the witnesses in a public place.

The most general objection to reliance on the police for booking and investigation is that it needlessly prolongs their forceful encounter with a person. Once away from the scene of a crime, the exigencies of time and place and circumstance that dictated their conduct there no longer control. While they may have to remove a person to prevent renewal of a disturbance or assure his availability later or for some other reason, removal *from* the scene need not be followed by removal *to* a police station. Out of long habit we treat the "trip to the stationhouse" as a part of an arrest. The more obvious course, however, would be to secure a person's release from police custody as quickly as possible, both to allow the police to attend to their peacekeeping duties and to replace the use of force with governmental authority more consistent with our respect for personal freedom and dignity and more likely to advance the needs of criminal process.

At the level of explicit authorization, we have understood that distinction and denied the police general investigative authority. There is no reason why they should acquire that authority automatically as a consequence of an arrest except when it is necessarily incidental to their peacekeeping function.* The courts have met the problem of supervising the investigative activities of the police by upholding their authority to investigate but imposing standards appropriate to an entirely different mode of performance. The Supreme Court has required, for example, that before the police question someone who is in custody, they advise him that he need not answer their questions, that his answers may be used against him, and so forth.[10] Taken at face value and given the weight that the Court's discussion seemed to intend, these so-called "Miranda warnings" would transform police questioning into a magisterial inquest. Similarly, the Court held that the police may not conduct a lineup unless defense counsel is present or there is some other assurance of fairness and impartiality.[11] The police, understandably, have not been able or indeed very willing to play a magisterial role in an encounter with someone whom they have just arrested; and, it may be added, even their best efforts are not likely to be convincing to someone in that situation. Out of that dilemma have arisen insoluble conflicts

*The lack of a functional connection between the authority of the police to arrest and their investigative authority is most evident when they arrest someone for a crime committed in the past, entirely outside the line of their peacekeeping duties. So long as they have probable cause to believe that person has committed a (serious) crime in the past, they can arrest him at any time, whatever he is then doing.

which look like inconsistencies of constitutional doctrine or conflicts of values, but often are attributable most of all to practical inability of the police to respond as we wish. The plain solution, instead of trying harder to make the police not act like police, is to assign the work now done at the police station to another agency which has responsibilities and characteristics more consistent with the way we want the work done.

We cannot have it both ways. If we intend to rely on "police questioning" as a deliberate prosecutorial technique to obtain evidence, then its close connection with an arrest is not to be regretted. A person's forcible removal from familiar surroundings helps to create the tense atmosphere in which such questioning succeeds; and since questioning takes place over an extended period of time, detention at the police station, even if it is unwilling, is essential. If that is *not* our intention, however, and our purpose is precisely to eliminate the coercive aspects of questioning in that atmosphere, as the Supreme Court has declared, we cannot expect to accomplish it merely by changing the rules.* It is a bootless effort to try to eliminate "police questioning" without eliminating questioning by police officers in a police station.

The same choice needs to be made about more diffuse benefits from the practice of detaining arrested persons at the station. The circumstances of the arrest or simply the circumstance of being arrested may lead a person to say something intended to exculpate him or ingratiate him with his captors; or he may converse as a way of "whistling in the dark." He may offer a "deal" or accept the offer of one, and

---

*One might prove the distinction between "police questioning" and simply asking questions by proposing that the police carry out their questioning by mailing to a person accused of a crime a list of questions, with a strongly worded request that he answer them if he chooses.

enable the police to clear a number of crimes even though prosecutions do not follow.* The period of arrest may be the time when an informer relationship is established for the future. More generally, the information that detectives pick up incidentally at the police station is a genuine part of their equipment as investigators. The police probably value unplanned benefits of this kind most of all. But their acceptability depends on their being unplanned. It makes too much of an untested suspicion of guilt to argue that if the police reasonably believe that a person has committed a crime, he is properly required to submit to police custody for some period, in the hope that the police will learn something.† As for the other kinds of investigative work that are now done at the police station, like searches, lineups, and body sampling, there is nothing to be gained, from any point of view, from the stationhouse atmosphere. A search or a blood test does not turn up more, nor is a witness's identification of someone in a lineup more certain, because the procedure is conducted forcefully. If force is used at all, it is an unhappy necessity.

---

*The benefit to him may be real and substantial. Or it may be no more than assurance that the police will not do what they have in any event no authority (and perhaps no intention) to do. As in comparable situations, the captive's desire for the favor of his captors may transcend the nice calculations he would make in another marketplace. The fact that such deals are made without clear benefit to the arrested person does not prove that the police are doing something improper—i.e., making threats—on their side of the transaction, although no doubt that is sometimes the case.

†The question may not be answered quite that easily for some. The French have faced up to the question (as we have not) and accepted that kind of exercise of state power in some circumstances. See Code de Procédure Pénale, articles 63, 77, allowing the police to detain someone temporarily (twenty-four or forty-eight hours) for investigative purposes.

The implication of the preceding discussion is that we should separate clearly the peacekeeping and emergency assistance functions of the police from investigative and prosecutorial functions which are not incidental to the former and do not require the same characteristics. It does not occur to us to conduct a criminal trial at the place where the crime occurred or to give the jury not more than thirty minutes (not to say thirty seconds) to reach a verdict. We do not require judges to demonstrate their marksmanship as a condition of office, or even to do twenty pushups. It is just as foolish to ask the police to behave as if they were magistrates. That means on the one hand that we should not impose on them standards of judicial behavior which they (and we) must ignore in practice if they are to do the work we want them to do. And on the other hand, we should not ask (or allow) them to perform work to which we seriously want those standards applied.

The principle of separation is evident. The responsibilities of the police should be limited to those tasks that we want performed swiftly, on the scene, and with force if it is necessary. Most of their work and their major responsibilities presently conform to that description. Some of the work that now is assigned to them as crime fighters does not and should be reassigned elsewhere. No doubt, it is easier to state the principle than to apply it. In one large respect, its application is easy. Having made an arrest in any circumstances, the police should have no authority to take the person to the police station. They should take him directly before other officials, who are responsible for whatever further steps are proper in furtherance of a criminal prosecution. If that single change were seriously made, it would have large consequences.* Conscientious insistence that the

---

*The qualification that the change be made seriously is important. After the Supreme Court restricted "custodial interrogation" at the

police not abuse their unique authority on the street and redefinition of their role so that they would not be responsible for crime except insofar as it was an aspect of their responsibility for preserving peace and order would be needed to implement the distinction between arrest and investigation in other respects.

The obvious question is where to assign the investigative and prosecutorial work that the police do now. There is no well-defined institution in our society that will serve. But in broad outline, the conception of such an office is easy to state; the standard against which that kind of police work is always measured is the judgment of "a neutral and detached magistrate."[12] We need, then, to establish the office of a magisterial investigator, or investigating magistrate, whose responsibility for investigating and preparing a case for prosecution is distinct from the work of the police. There is an investigating magistracy in most countries. In this country, the concept may suggest to many persons "inquisitorial" techniques of criminal process that we reject. As an initial matter, however, the establishment of such an agency authorized to do only what the police are already authorized to do would be a clear improvement. As between the police station and a public agency with the neutral, nonforceful trappings of the judiciary, the choice is obvious. So too, the choice is obvious between removal of a person to a police station, where he must submit to police officers whose primary authority, training, and identity are bound up with the use of force, and his immediate release into the custody of a judicial officer trained for the tasks assigned to him. How such an official might proceed is described in Chapter 6.

---

police station, it was reported that police in the District of Columbia were taking the "scenic route" to the station house and furiously questioning the arrested person in the back seat on the way. That was hardly what the Supreme Court had in mind.

The harmful effects of our reliance on the police to perform tasks inappropriate to their qualifications or authority are evident long after their direct involvement in a case has ended. Not the least of our difficulties in criminal process has been the absence of an official agency on which we are prepared to rely for the initial stages of a prosecution. By transferring investigative and prosecutorial functions not directly related to peacekeeping to a proper agency, we shall not only rationalize the work of the police. We shall also be able to reconstruct the criminal process in ways more likely to achieve its purposes. That is the subject of the next chapters.

3

PROSECUTION

    This and the next two chapters describe the course of
a criminal prosecution in this country: its initiation
and development and its conclusion by a plea of guilty or a
trial. The investigation and prosecution of a crime are
separated and entrusted to different institutions: the police
on the one hand and, primarily, the prosecutor's office and
the private bar (and public defender's office) on the other.
The separation is not supported by any general epistemolo-
gical theory or methodology. In our ordinary affairs we do
not usually isolate our effort to learn information relevant to
a decision from the effort to decide, although we may
approach an especially difficult decision by explicitly weigh-
ing the pros and cons or preparing lists of reasons on each
side. The collection and organization of relevant information
and the dismissal of what is not relevant are themselves what
constitute deciding. Nor is it typical of the criminal process

in particular that the functions of learning and proving the facts of a crime are separated from one another; in most countries they are not.

Prosecution is characterized by a division between the two "sides" of a case. Once a person has been accused, he is formally a "defendant." Thereafter until his guilt is finally determined, everything happens within the theoretical structure of an "adversary system," which gives primary responsibility for the conduct of the case to the prosecutor and defense counsel. Usually, reference to an adversary system conveys in particular the government's burden "to shoulder the entire load" and prove the defendant's guilt without assistance from him.[1] What is not generally re-marked is that the functions of prosecution and defense are not only opposed; they are complementary. If one is en-larged, the other diminishes.

The prosecutor is described as an "officer of the court" and exhorted to see that "justice is done." But his duty is defined primarily by his role as an adversary. It does not ordinarily include an obligation to intervene in behalf of a less able or diligent opponent. He is not expected to round up absent witnesses for the defendant or help prepare them for trial; he does not help a bumbling defense counsel destroy the credibility of one of the government's witnesses. Were he to do anything like that, except in an extraordinary situation, it would be contrary not only to the assumptions of the trial process but also to professional behavior. Defense counsel is also supposed to be an "officer of the court." Were he deliberately to intervene in favor of the prosecution to see that "justice is done," in any ordinary situation his conduct would constitute evidence, and very likely proof, that he was incompetent.

The defendant's lawyer is an independent actor who has final authority to decide whether and how to act over a broad range; no other person reviews his decisions and ensures that he performs competently. If carelessly or foolishly he does not carry out tasks within his responsibility, that usually means that they are not performed at all. Our reliance on defense counsel is based on the assumption that so far as his role is concerned, the defendant's interest in avoiding a conviction coincides with our own interest in the proper functioning of the process. Reliance to so large an extent is nonetheless remarkable. We generally leave it to the defendant to choose—and pay—his lawyer; counsel is provided for indigent defendants only because they are unable to provide for themselves. We assume that the abilities of lawyers vary, as do their fees. Having no alternative within an adversary system, the criminal process accommodates as well as can be expected the respective demands of criminal justice and the private practice of criminal law, which do not always run along parallel tracks. If defense lawyers fairly proclaim sometimes how well they meet the needs of criminal justice, it is true also that throughout the process, criminal justice bends to meet the demands they make of it.

Once the police have made an arrest and completed their procedures at the police station, the investigation of most crimes for practical purposes is over. Evidence of a crime, like other events, usually is obtained most readily when and where it happened. The police gather evidence at the scene of the crime and track down available leads as part of their initial response. If it is unclear whether a crime was committed (as in many cases of personal injury or death, when the people involved all knew one another) or which of several identified suspects committed it, the police will dispose of the question promptly and end the investigation. If a crime clearly was committed but there are no good leads to the criminal, the investigation ends when the police, having performed their peacekeeping function, leave the scene. In those few cases which the police do investigate intensively, there too an arrest ordinarily signals that they have finished investigating. The standard formula used to announce that an investigation is about to end is "An arrest is near."

So far as the police are concerned, an arrest carries out their responsibility for the criminal aspects of a case. Nothing that happens thereafter affects their accomplishment. They are angry and frustrated if a person whom they have arrested is returned to the street without being prosecuted; but they do not regard that as their failure (any more than a prosecutor regards it as his failure that a man whom he convicts is not reformed in prison). Having made the arrest and satisfied themselves that they have an accurate account of the event, the police "clear" the case. The arresting officer, or in a more complicated case one of the detectives who worked on it, writes a report which contains a brief description of the crime, the police response, and enough evidentiary detail to support the arrest.

The police prepare the report for their own purposes. It is an internal memorandum intended to justify the arrest and clear the case, not to establish the defendant's guilt in any legally significant way. It has no independent evidentiary value. Nevertheless, in the vast majority of cases, all the information on which proof of guilt and a conviction ultimately depend is contained or indicated either in the police report or documents like witnesses' statements that accompany it in the police file. Thus, a police officer who captures a purse snatcher on the street often is himself the main witness for the prosecution. The crime will be proved by the victim's testimony that the purse is hers and was taken from her forcibly, her identification of the man if she had a chance to look at him, and above all the officer's testimony that he apprehended the man at the scene with the purse in his possession. If the victim is seriously injured or should die, medical testimony to establish the fact will be needed. But that is about all. If the arrest is made later instead of at the time and place of the crime, the basis of identification will be more elaborate; for example, testimony of other witnesses who saw the incident may be needed. The names of the witnesses will probably have been obtained as soon as the police arrived on the scene.

The nature of the investigative function, which is tied to immediate peacekeeping activities, and the plain fact that most crimes which are not cleared quickly and conclusively are not cleared at all have the effect that almost always information about a crime is as definite and the sources of information are as certain as they ever will be within a very short time after the arrest, which usually means very shortly after the crime was committed. The doubts that remain are not likely to depend on unknown information which further inquiry will reveal so much as on the legal significance of known facts or information available from known sources. One would expect, therefore, that once the police have completed their investigation, the criminal process would move swiftly to a conclusion. In view of the consequences for the defendant and the community both, only in rare cases and for compelling reasons should it be slowed.

An actual prosecution follows a different schedule. Having been arrested, a person is not then formally accused of a crime for several weeks or, it may be, months. Once he has been accused, months pass, punctuated occasionally by legal proceedings that do not affect the substance of the case against him. If after months of inaction he is convicted, the judgment depends in all likelihood on the evidence in the police file from the beginning. In the rare event that the case goes to trial, probably no evidence is presented that was not available more readily and more credibly when the police turned the case over to the prosecutor.

The case of Rodney McCoy illustrates this pattern. Three men committed an armed robbery at Benson's Jewelry Store in downtown Washington, D.C. As soon as they left the store, the police were called. Within minutes a "lookout" was broadcast on the police radio. About thirty minutes later a police officer stopped McCoy and another man who fit the description in the lookout nineteen blocks from Benson's. He searched them and found a gun and two trays of rings in a plastic bag. The men were immediately brought back to Benson's, where the owner of the store identified them as two of the robbers. All of that happened within less than an hour after the holdup.

Whether McCoy was guilty or innocent, there was no evidence that was not available then and there. There were other persons in the store when the holdup occurred; whether they would corroborate or refute the owner's identification of McCoy as a robber, the sooner their testimony was reliably obtained the better. If McCoy had an alibi or an innocent explanation for his possession of the rings, he was much more likely to be able to establish it then than later on. If he was provably guilty, he should have been convicted and sentenced; and if not, he should have been released.

In the actual case, McCoy was detained in jail for more than three months before he was officially accused. He was then accused of twelve crimes (individual assaults and robberies of each of the persons in the store), the maximum penalty for which was imprisonment for several lifetimes. He remained in jail for another three months and was then released into the custody of his mother. He was tried for the crimes at Benson's two years and seven months after they occurred. After a two-day trial, during which seven of the charges against him were dropped or dismissed, the remaining charges went to the jury, which found him guilty of one charge of armed robbery. Two months later, close to three years after the crime, McCoy was sentenced. He was given a suspended sentence of imprisonment for two to six years and was placed on probation for three years.[2]

The delay in McCoy's case was extreme.* But the pattern is familiar. The general circumstances which accounted for the time lost are present in almost every prosecution for a serious crime because they are part of the process itself.

The police are allowed to retain custody of a person after his arrest only long enough to complete the procedures at the station described in the preceding chapter. If they conclude that he should not be prosecuted, they can release him without more, and the criminal matter ends there. If they believe that the prosecution should go forward, in some cases of minor crimes they may release him at the police station with instructions to appear before a magistrate the next day. More commonly, they deliver him to a magistrate who has authority to order him held in custody while the criminal charges are determined or to release him on bail.

The detention of a person in jail or the imposition of conditions on his liberty while a criminal prosecution is pending does not affect the form of the prosecution. Our bail practices, however, are among the most difficult to justify of the criminal process. Theoretically, a person is detained or conditions are imposed on his liberty if there is reason to believe that he might otherwise flee. Bail is often

*Much of it was due to the government's appeal from an adverse ruling of the court before the case went to trial.

used, however, simply as a means of detaining someone because of fear that he will commit crimes before he is brought to trial. Since the same factors which indicate that a defendant might be dangerous also probably indicate in a general way that he may not appear as required, it is not difficult for a magistrate to set conditions of bail which he knows the defendant cannot meet; and in fact dangerousness is regarded as a relevant consideration more or less openly.

The most common condition of bail is a bond in some amount, which the defendant forfeits if he does not appear as required. That practice supports the business of professional bonding, by which the defendant pays the bondsman a fee in return for which the bondsman undertakes to pay the amount of the bond if the defendant flees. Most of the time, the bondsman does nothing to earn his fee except apply his statistical information about the defendant's reliability when he decides whether or not to take the defendant as a client. Obviously, the bondsman's undertaking does nothing to keep the defendant from fleeing. In some jurisdictions a defendant is allowed to pay a small percentage of the amount of the bond into court; unlike a bondsman's fee, the payment into court is returned to him if he appears as required. That alternative is superior in every respect to professional bonding, which continues, however, to exist in most states.

Defendants who are not released on bail are kept in jails, which are usually among the worst facilities of our prison systems. The conditions of most jails are appalling. There is, furthermore, good reason to believe that a defendant who is detained in jail is more likely to be found guilty at trial and likely to be sentenced more severely than one who has not. Even if we were to assume that a person who is accused of a crime is probably guilty, there is no justification for allowing detention *in order that* the defendant may be tried and punished to become a determinant of the outcome of the trial and the severity of punishment. The injustice, not to mention the indecency, of pretrial detention as it is presently imposed is evident. It is punishment before we have established that punishment is deserved; and it is punishment which has the curious effect of increasing the chance that one will be found to deserve to be punished.

So long as the criminal process includes delays of months after the investigation of a crime is substantially complete, there is no way to resolve the conflicts in our bail practice. Once we have concluded that someone probably is a dangerous criminal and that he will be prosecuted, we shall not easily release him immediately into the community for so long a period. So far as we can do so without too much public strain on our commitment to justice and professions of respect for the individual, we shall continue to detain many persons accused of serious crimes. If the period of detention continues to be as long as it is, detention in decent conditions cannot be more than a theoretical ideal. Not only would the cost of decent conditions be more than we are likely to spend for the group of persons involved; without regard to cost, prolonged detention with no purpose except eventual trial and conviction is likely to become indecent whatever resources we might provide. When we do not detain a defendant, we shall probably continue to use the empty form of a bail proceeding, which gives at least the appearance of minimizing the danger to society which delay creates.

According to our ordinary principles, the burden of the societal objectives served by the criminal process should be shared instead of imposed largely on the persons who are accused. One way to share the burden of delay between accusation and judgment would be to limit detention before trial to a very brief period—ordinarily no more than a few days. Were trials delayed longer, the community would have to bear the burden of whatever danger, whether flight or crimes, was created.* It does not seem unreasonable to suppose also that the conditions of detention for so brief a period might be made decent. Despite constant criticism of our bail practices, we have not improved them very much. We are not likely to do so unless the criminal process itself is transformed.

The delivery of an arrested person to a magistrate terminates the arrest and with it official police responsibility. At the same time or soon afterwards, a police officer or the victim of the crime at the request of the police files a complaint which initiates the prosecution. The complaint is nothing more than an accusation that someone has committed a crime, specified by bare details like the time, place, and victim. Formally, a complaint is the means by which a private person informs the government about a crime. Since it is supposed to start an investigation, not signal the end of one, it does not have to contain evidence to prove its charges; but it has to be made seriously, usually under oath. Once the duty of the police to investigate crime was established, the complaint became largely superfluous. We all know how to call the police; but few of us know where or how to file a complaint. When we want to report a crime we report it to the police, who respond on their own authority and do not need a complaint to act. Usually, therefore, a complaint is filed simply as a formality. One police officer may file complaints to cover a number of arrests made by other officers; as complainant, he swears to his belief in the

*Extraordinary civil commitment procedures are available outside the criminal process for detention of persons who are believed to be extremely dangerous. They are rarely used at present to detain someone who has been accused of a crime because it is so much easier to resort to bail, which does not require the same proof of dangerousness and gives the person far less opportunity to resist detention.

accusations on the basis of the police reports prepared by others.*

Accompanied by evidence of probable cause, the complaint is sufficient to authorize holding the defendant while the prosecutor decides whether or not to go forward with a prosecution. But it is not itself an accusation to which the defendant must (or can) respond. In the federal courts and some states, the formal accusation is contained in an indictment made by a grand jury of private citizens. The grand jury was originally an investigative and informing body which the English kings' itinerant ministers of justice summoned to inform them about local crimes. In the American colonies it became a protection against the government; insistence on grand juries was part of the colonial struggle for home rule. So long as the community was small and serious crimes were rare and notorious, it made sense to rely on a body of ordinary citizens to investigate and accuse. Once the "local community" became a crowded, anonymous city, ordinary citizens lacked the time or inclination or awareness to investigate crimes; and there was little reason for them to do so if the police had investigated and made an arrest already. The decision to prosecute was more appropriately assigned to a professional bureaucracy than to an *ad hoc* body of laymen.

England, where the grand jury originated, abolished it in 1933 (and had generally abandoned it much earlier). In this country, the right to an indictment by a grand jury is

*In some jurisdictions, the police consult with the prosecutor before the complaint is filed. If that is the practice, the prosecutor's bureaucratic decision whether to prosecute and if so for what crime is made then; and if the decision is not to prosecute, no complaint will be filed. Since the complaint is a formality in any event and requires no official action, the substance of the prosecutor's decision is the same whether it is made before or after the complaint is filed. See pages 58–59.

preserved by the federal Constitution and some state constitutions.[3] But except in the most extraordinary circumstances, it has little practical importance. The grand jury gladly relies on the prosecutor's recommendations. He decides what evidence is presented to it and advises it about the law. The prospective defendant does not ordinarily appear and may not even be aware of the proceeding. If he has been arrested, of course, he knows that an indictment is likely to follow.

Where the grand jury has been eliminated, the prosecutor prepares the accusation, called an "information," which is usually subject one way or another to judicial approval. Commonly he is required to present evidence to support the accusation at a "preliminary hearing" or "preliminary examination" at which the defendant also can appear and present evidence. The presiding magistrate may exercise more independent judgment than grand jurors do. But it is still the prosecutor's show. He does not have to convince the magistrate that the defendant is guilty, but only that there is enough evidence of guilt to call for a trial. Rules of evidence and adversary procedures that constrain the prosecutor at trial are mostly inapplicable at the hearing, where the magistrate is likely to be impatient with drawn-out, technical arguments from the defense. Unless there is no substantial evidence of guilt at all, it is easier for the magistrate to sustain the accusation and push the question of guilt forward than to reject it and take the burden of error on himself. The defendant's lawyer sometimes tries to enlarge the hearing. He may cross-examine the prosecutor's witnesses or summon witnesses of his own to learn about the case or gain some hoped-for advantage at trial; or he may prolong the hearing to convince the prosecutor that the case will be long and difficult and should be negotiated, or just to show his client how hard he is working. But almost never does he or anyone else expect that the magistrate will reject the accusation. More often than not, defense counsel waives his client's right to a preliminary hearing because it would serve no purpose or simply because he has not yet received any part of his fee.

Important as the formal accusation is within the theoretical structure of a prosecution, the crime or crimes actually charged in the indictment or information are immaterial except in one respect. The defendant can be convicted of any crime less serious than the crimes charged and contained within them; but he cannot be convicted of any more serious crime. This principle that a defendant can be convicted of the crime(s) charged or "lesser included offenses" means from the prosecutor's point of view that the defendant should be charged with the most serious crimes that the evidence will reasonably support. In a case of homicide, for example, a defendant who is accused of murder in the first degree can be convicted, according to the evidence, of that crime, murder in the second degree, manslaughter, attempted murder, assault in various degrees, and perhaps other crimes as well. On that basis, prosecutors commonly assume that if a defendant is accused of second-degree murder he will not be convicted of anything more serious than manslaughter, since he would have been charged with first-degree murder if the case were at all a "good" one.

The practice of "charging up" because you can convict "down" but not "up" is the more rational bureaucratically because that early in the process probably no one believes that the final outcome will depend on a precise evaluation of the evidence. The more likely assumption is that if the defendant is convicted, the crime(s) will be determined by negotiation between the prosecutor and defense counsel, who will make a general assessment of the evidence and various tactical considerations rather than evaluate closely precise distinctions among the possible crimes. Furthermore, the "higher" the accusation, the greater is the appearance of a bargain for the defendant when an agreement is reached. It is often said that prosecutors deliberately charge "up" in order to gain a bargaining advantage. While it is true that more serious charges make a bargain more likely, that explanation is superfluous. Having in mind that a negotiated plea of guilty is the probable outcome, the prosecutor has no reason at the outset to make a difficult calculation of what crime the defendant actually committed and should be convicted for. Although in theory the indictment or information is a solemn accusation, in practice it is not meant to reflect that kind of careful determination.

With his task so defined, it is easy to understand how the prosecutor works. The police report ordinarily is a sufficient source of all the information he needs. If the police have omitted relevant information it is probably doubts and details that can be disregarded if all that is at stake is the most serious plausible accusation. Unless the police report on its face reveals an inconsistency or barrier to conviction, the prosecutor accepts the general conclusion of the police without making an independent investigation or evaluation of the evidence. If he has to present evidence to a grand jury or magistrate, he may leave it to his secretary to read the report and summon the appropriate witnesses, who are often the police officers who wrote the report. If he can proceed without review by a grand jury or magistrate, he will read the report, perhaps interview the officers briefly and informally, and, unless something appears out of the ordinary, be satisfied.

When the prosecutor makes his decision is largely a matter of convenience. All that is necessary is that at some point before the defendant is formally accused, he review the evidence gathered by the police closely enough to avoid manifest error and to characterize the crime legally in general terms. He may do that before or after the complaint is filed, before the grand jury's or magistrate's hearing, or, proceeding "by the seat of his pants," in the course of the hearing itself. It is pointless to criticize prosecutors for making charging decisions that way. Were it the rule that a defendant could not be convicted of any crime "up" or "down," but only the crime(s) charged, there would be a different kind of prosecutorial decision. Such a rule, which would require the most careful initial determination of guilt and appropriate penalty, would transform the entire criminal process and not merely the accusation.

Despite all the attention given to the accusatory procedure, it accomplishes little except to transform the conclusions of the police into a formal accusation which submits the defendant to the criminal process; an arrest becomes a prosecution. The law gives great attention to the manner of the transformation and allows a long time for it to be accomplished. The process of determining guilt or punishment is not advanced. The state does not learn more than it knew or make certain what was previously uncertain. After the defendant is accused, the state has not yet seriously begun the task of deciding whether it should convict him of any crime or what his punishment should be. He still does not have before him a serious assertion by the state of which he can take account.

The unimportance of the accusation is confirmed at the arraignment, at which the defendant is required to plead guilty or not guilty. The proceeding is encumbered by formalities that suggest its theoretical importance. The defendant is expected to appear and plead personally. Rules of procedure and judicial decisions specify the precise formula by which he must be asked for his plea. The actual conduct of the arraignment is a meaningless, trivial ritual which is manifestly so regarded by everyone who participates in it. Arraignments are conducted in a crowded courtroom bustling with defendants and lawyers. The clerk of the court may read the charges and ask the defendant for his plea while the judge does something else. The defendant automatically pleads "Not guilty." That, of course, is the only thing he can do given the nature of the accusation. Were he to do anything else, the proceeding would stop while everyone assured himself that the defendant understood what was happening. There is no expectation that the defendant will plead guilty at the arraignment. He does not gain anything by doing so, nor does anyone regard it as his moral or legal duty to do so whether he is guilty or not. The prosecutor does not regard a plea of not guilty as a challenge to the state's case; he does not know yet what the state's case is.

So the prosecution is begun. One can state the matter as one likes: since the initial proceedings accomplish nothing, no one takes them seriously; since no one takes them seriously, they accomplish nothing. By the time the defendant is arraigned, a month or more has passed since he was arrested.

At the arraignment or soon afterwards a tentative date for the trial is chosen without much attention to the particular circumstances of the case. In *McCoy,* for example, the date originally scheduled for the trial was five months after the arraignment (which was already four months after the crime); it was of no relevance that all the evidence had been readily available for a long time. When the trial date is set, neither the prosecutor nor defense counsel has studied the case or made any significant preparation for trial. The judge who will try the case knows nothing about it and, if there is more than one judge to whom the case may be assigned, has probably not even been picked. The trial date is based mostly on the convenience of the lawyers, which may include not only other professional obligations that cannot be postponed but also a generally busy schedule this week or that, a long-planned vacation, and almost anything else that defense counsel wants to mention. Courtesy toward a member of the same profession prevents the prosecutor or the judge or clerk who prepares the trial schedule from examining closely the reasons for delay. The prosecutor is similarly indulged; but usually he can be more flexible because the case can be reassigned for trial to any of several prosecutors and, in any event, the time requested by defense counsel is sufficient. The court itself may rule out certain weeks for a Christmas or spring holiday or a judicial convention, to accommodate a lightened summer workload, or whatever.

Within the broadest limits it is of small importance to anyone how fast the process goes forward. If the defendant demands a speedy trial, which he is constitutionally guaranteed, he may have it. But it would not be a denial of his constitutional right if the trial were delayed for several months. Likely as not, his own lawyer delays the trial as much as anyone. Usually the defendant is glad to have the trial put off. Evidence of guilt is rarely improved by time; hope springs eternal and not always in vain. If as individuals the prosecutor and judge disapprove the delay, in their professional roles they are constrained by the system within which they function, which regards a delay of several months as normal. For all that, the trial date is only tentative. Intervening events, including special demands on the lawyers or judge, may require that it be rescheduled. "Continuances" are freely granted even though everyone knows that in fact a trial is unlikely and the process of negotiation that leads to a plea of guilty will not begin until the delays are over and a firm date for trial is imminent.

In a busy prosecutor's office, the lawyer who reviewed the police report and prepared the accusation, and if it was necessary presented evidence to the grand jury or magistrate, probably has no further connection with the case. After the arraignment, the case is assigned to another lawyer in the trial division who is responsible for it thereafter, during the period before trial as well as during the negotiation of a plea or the trial. Most likely, when the file of the case reaches his office, he will not do more than glance briefly at the papers, more out of curiosity than anything else, before putting the file away with a note on his calendar to review the case a few days before the trial date. Defense counsel may make a request or file a motion in court that requires the prosecutor to look at the case during the pretrial period. Otherwise, unless it has some feature that is out of the ordinary, there is no reason why he should begin to work on it months before a trial is scheduled, before he has any idea whether it will go to trial at all. A prosecutor's calendar may list half a dozen ordinary cases—unspectacular robberies, housebreakings, assaults, narcotics offenses, even murder or rape—for trial in the same week, several on the same day. Since most of them will be resolved by a plea of guilty before trial, the calendar is realistic; if it turns out that more than one case actually is ready for trial at the same time, he can postpone one of them for a day or two or find another prosecutor who is able to try it.

The defense counsel theoretically is in a different situation. He is not expected to study the case or to prepare at all before the defendant enters a plea. Unlike the accusation, the plea of not guilty need not be factually based even in theory. Nor is there usually an opportunity before the defendant pleads to test the legal basis for the prosecution. After the arraignment, therefore, defense counsel is given time to prepare the defense and the initiative passes to him. The range of his responsibilities during the pretrial period is large. They include review of the procedural aspects of the prosecution to see whether there is any ground for dismissal of the accusation independent of the factual issue of the defendant's guilt, investigation of the facts of the crime to uncover gaps in the evidence against the defendant and to develop evidence in his favor, and challenge of arrangements for the trial that might be worked out more favorably to the defendant. In theory, defense counsel is expected to examine all the decisions of the prosecutor and challenge any of them that are incorrect legally or take undue advantage of his client. Finally, like the prosecutor, when and if the time comes he has to prepare the case for trial. The reason most commonly given for the long pretrial period is the importance of these aspects of the defense to the proper functioning of the adversary system and the complexity of the issues that may arise. In fact, in order to maintain the large number of cases on which the successful private practice of criminal law (or maintenance of a public defender's office) depends, defense counsel must dispose of most cases routinely and give each of them only a few hours of his attention.

Prosecutions typically are as banal as the crimes themselves. Legal objections to the jurisdiction of the court or to the selection of the grand jury or the manner of its deliberations, objections on the ground that the statute of limitations or the defendant's constitutional protection against double jeopardy bars a prosecution, or other similar challenges can be made during the pretrial period. Grounds for such objections are rare. All of them raise a question about the ordinary procedures of the prosecutor's office, which simply as a matter of professional competence generally complies with the legal requirements of a prosecution. The legal arguments that surround such an issue when it does arise may be intricate; and it is sometimes true that a particularly skilled, careful lawyer will perceive a basis for challenge that is not at once apparent. Nevertheless, the issues arise extremely infrequently. In an ordinary case defense counsel does not spend half an hour considering legal objections of this kind. Were there even an apparent basis for such objections very often, it would indicate that the prosecutor's office was incompetent.

A great deal is said about defense counsel's duty to investigate the crime in his client's behalf. Thorough, imaginative investigation may make the difference between a favorable or unfavorable verdict if the case goes to trial and the facts are unclear or legally ambiguous (or, obviously, much more rarely if the defendant is entirely and unequivocally innocent). Just the same, defense counsel's independent investigation of the facts usually consists mainly, if not exclusively, of one or more interviews with his client. Routine crimes present few avenues which defense counsel might explore. Brought into a case weeks after a crime was committed, in the cold tracks of the police, a busy defense lawyer needs the goad of extraordinary circumstances to set out on another inquiry of his own rather than rely on what the defendant can tell him and what he can learn from the prosecutor. He will go further only if there are substantial indications that exculpatory evidence was overlooked.

Far from questioning that narrow conception of defense counsel's responsibility, institutional arrangements support it. His professional arenas are his office and the courthouse, not the street. He does not have at his disposal an agency like the police to carry out requests for on-scene investigations or pursue uncertain leads. He does not have the prosecutor's formal or informal means for summoning witnesses to his office for an interview; if he confronts them at their own homes or work places, too often he finds them hostile or suspicious, already allied with the prosecution and unwilling to discuss the case. He knows that whatever his client says now, when the trial is imminent he will probably plead guilty and render any investigative efforts useless.

Until quite recently, it was generally assumed that evidence of the defendant's guilt which the police assembled was a part of the government's case and "belonged" to it in a quite literal sense, which made its disclosure to the defense an act of generosity rather than a requirement. Unlike the prosecutor, who received investigative reports automatically, defense counsel was obliged either to make a formal motion in court for "discovery," which was limited to certain kinds of evidence, or to rely on the prosecutor's good will. When that was not enough, the only course open to defense counsel was painstakingly to retread ground which the police had already covered, to find out what they and the prosecutor already knew.

Prosecutors now open their files to defense counsel more often, and rules of court have provided for extensive disclosure of the government's case. But in the federal courts and most of the state courts "discovery" is still incomplete. The items that most often are not covered are also the most important: names of witnesses and their statements to the police. The main arguments against disclosure are that witnesses will be intimidated or that they or the defendant will be encouraged to commit perjury if he knows before trial who they are and what they will say.[4] Guilty (as well as innocent) defendants, of course, frequently have that information without being told. In fact, there are a number of jurisdictions where discovery of witnesses and their testimony is allowed; there is nothing in the experience of those jurisdictions to support such fears. Resistance to discovery is based less on such arguments than on a "feel-ing" of unfairness that the adversary system engenders. If there really are two sides, why should one side do all the work? In the context of criminal justice, the question makes no sense.

For all these reasons, investigation by defense counsel during the pretrial period seldom means more than an effort to learn what evidence the government has against his client. The simple way to accomplish that objective is to reject the assumption that evidence belongs to one side or the other. In view of our reliance on defense counsel to conduct the defense, the critical question ought not to be "How much of the evidence does the state have to reveal?" but "How can we be certain that defense counsel studies and makes full use of all that he is given?" We do not require defense counsel to disclose the fruits of his efforts to the prosecutor for reasons having to do with the defendant's right to resist the state's process against him; those reasons do not apply to the state's obligation to disclose what it knows to him.

The remaining pretrial responsibility of defense counsel is to ensure the fairness of the trial itself. In an ordinary case, the time and place and scope of the trial present no special difficulty. Questions occasionally arise. If the defendant has been accused of more than one crime or two or more defendants have been accused together, the joint trial may be opposed. The defendant may prefer a different location for trial, to obtain a more neutral jury or for his own or witnesses' convenience. Such issues are raised by a motion in court that the prosecutor can oppose if he wishes. The rules excluding from trial evidence obtained in violation of the defendant's constitutional rights have led to the practice of considering before trial objections to evidence on constitu-tional grounds. Motions to "suppress" evidence are somewhat more common than other motions concerning the conduct of the trial; but they are still infrequent. Sometimes a motion can be decided by examining the document that authorized a police action; evidence seized in a search, for example, might be challenged on the ground that the search warrant on which the police relied was invalid. More often, the police action is not based on a specific authorization, and there is a hearing to consider the manner in which the evidence was obtained. Usually the hearing consists mainly, if not exclusively, of the opposed testimony of the defendant and the police officer(s) whose conduct is challenged. Within the adversary system, which makes even a response to police illegality dependent on the initiative of defense counsel, the hearing, months after the event in issue, is too often a ''swearing contest'' between the police and the defendant, which the judge must resolve as he can. Motions to suppress evidence sometimes have a perceptible effect on the outcome of a prosecution. But, unsurprisingly in the circumstances, judges rarely decide in favor of the defendant unless the conduct of the police was flagrantly unlawful; and they are the less likely to do so if the evidence at stake appears to be critical to the government's case.

No one claims that defense counsel really needs the long period after the arraignment to accomplish these tasks. If in rare cases preparation of the defense requires time and energy, in the vast majority defense counsel gives it little of either until a few days before the trial is scheduled. Lacking a means of distinguishing among cases independently of defense counsel, we allow in every instance a delay that is merited in exceedingly few. Even so, having the differences among defense counsel in mind, we have in most cases far less assurance than we should that all the tasks have been performed properly. Allowing the abstract principle that the defendant should have a meaningful opportunity to defend himself to overshadow other requirements of the criminal process, we have at the same time been remarkably sloppy about ensuring the practical realization of the principle.

The passage of months before an accusation is ready to be resolved cannot be dismissed as a regrettable but incidental aspect of our criminal process. Even were the matter of punishment not involved, none of us would easily accept so long a delay in finding the facts about a private matter where the accuracy and credibility of the results counted for so much. We should not collect all the information and then so casually and routinely postpone making up our minds. If there is a change in the evidence during the pretrial period, it is likely to become less rather than more convincing. Not only may witnesses' recollections become fuzzy and confused; they may also harden into simple patterns which eliminate troublesome but significant ambiguities of detail. The needless separation of crime and punishment makes the penalty when it finally is imposed more like the gratuitous infliction of harm. In the case of Rodney McCoy, for example, what could have been our explanation for the penalty if, instead of receiving a suspended sentence, he had been sent to prison a few weeks before his twenty-third birthday because of a crime committed when he was twenty?

Yet by allowing the delay we are assured of nothing. Most of the time, when the trial date finally approaches, the basis for convicting the defendant is the same as it was months before, probably within a few hours of the crime. For the government, the significant document is still the police report. For the defendant and his lawyer, what counts is what the defendant knows about the case. If there has been any further investigation or exchange of information or resolution of contested procedural issues, it could have been accomplished more credibly and reliably long before. Most likely, whatever has intervened, the so-called "pretrial" period will be brought to an end not by a trial, but by the defendant's plea of guilty.

4

GUILTY PLEAS

The scheduling of a trial is generally nothing more
than an elaborate charade. A date is chosen when the
prosecutor and defense counsel will be free to try the case, a
judge and a courtroom will be available, witnesses will be
present, and so forth, as if everyone expected that there
would actually be a trial. As the lawyers and judge (and the
defendant, if he has been prosecuted before) know, there
probably will not. When all postponements of the trial are
over and the scheduled date is imminent, in eight or nine
cases out of ten the defendant pleads guilty and the case is
taken off the court's calendar. Were the ''trial'' date set with
a guilty plea in mind, any date would be as good as any other.
The prosecutor and defense counsel usually need only a few
minutes to arrange the plea; and it takes just a few minutes
more for the defendant to enter it in court.

On any fair account of our actual practices, conviction

by guilty plea is normal and a trial the exception. This reversal of the theoretical and actual models of our criminal process is the more striking because we are so fond of proclaiming it a mark of our civilization that the government is required to prove a person's guilt without assistance from him, by "its own independent labors."[1] In fact, we rely on the defendant's formal admission of guilt far more than other countries, whose procedures we criticize because they are not based so fully on our conception of an adversary system. In view of the infrequency of a trial in this country, our insistence on the superiority of the trial model is somewhat lame.

The prevalence of guilty pleas has been obvious for a long time to anyone who has paid attention to actual criminal justice. But it is only in the past dozen years or so that it has attracted much public notice. The common explanation for departing from the trial model is the number of criminal cases; the burden on our resources, the courts in particular, of trying every case would be too great. But how seriously can one take a claimed preference which is ignored nine times out of ten because it costs too much? By ordinary standards, even the standards of government bureaucracy, many trial courts are not overworked (unless, of course, one's sole criterion is simply the number of cases "processed"). No increase in efficiency would enable the courts to try all defendants fully as a trial is now conceived; but guilty pleas are substituted for trials without reluctance, more than unpassable limitations of resources require. We are not without some choice in the administration of justice about how many criminal cases to accommodate and how to make the accommodation. Although in practice most cases are dismissed or disposed of by plea bargaining, almost never is it suggested, for example, that in order to conform to the trial model we ought to narrow the range of conduct that is declared criminal. We cannot explain our reliance on guilty pleas by observing that they dispose of a lot of cases and letting it go at that.

Despite our usual, predictable reliance on guilty pleas, no place is assigned for them in the formal structure of a prosecution. The defendant's decision to plead guilty is treated as if it were a surprise, an unplanned and unexpected departure from the normal course. The only provision for a defendant to plead is the initial arraignment, at which he routinely pleads not guilty to the government's *pro forma* accusation. The later plea of guilty to a serious accusation, worked out by negotiation between the prosecutor and defense counsel, is described as a "correction" of the earlier plea, as though the defendant having thought further about the matter had changed his mind. Formalities aside, however, the actual course of a prosecution is shaped from the beginning to make a guilty plea the natural outcome. The initial accusation vastly inflates the potential consequences of conviction, and no serious determination of what charges would be proper is made aside from the plea agreement. Consequently, there is the fullest scope for an unimpeded negotiation, which can extend to the whole range between the unreal maximum of the original accusation and the unlikely minimum of an acquittal. Ordinarily the defense is delivered fully into the hands of a private lawyer, whose professional livelihood depends on his *not* trying many cases. Public defenders' offices, whose lawyers defend the indigent, are similarly compelled; the resources allowed to the office are not enough for the trial of more than a small fraction of the cases assigned to it.

Guilty pleas are encouraged in other ways more explicitly. Courts in which several judges hear criminal cases may allow a defendant to choose the judge before whom he pleads guilty but give him no choice about the judge before whom the case would be tried. Since the judge who receives the plea or tries the case also imposes sentence, the defendant can hope for a lighter sentence if he pleads guilty before a judge who has a reputation for leniency; he can at least be sure of avoiding a judge who he believes would sentence him severely. Even when there is no opportunity for "judge shopping," one way or another judges let it be known that sentencing concessions are available to defendants who plead guilty.

Both lawyers in the case understand their regular duties to include negotiation of a plea. In that respect, defense counsel resembles lawyers in civil practice, who generally regard it as part of their duty to a client to avoid litigation. Although they perform ably for their clients by ordinary professional standards, many defense counsel lack the capacity to try a case and would admit the lack. While such an admission would be startling in the context of criminal practice because of the theoretical emphasis on a trial, in this also defense counsel resemble other lawyers. Most of the lawyers in large law firms are unable to try a case; they do not regard themselves as unprepared to serve their clients.

The prosecutor also enters negotiations routinely. On rare occasions he may want a specific benefit, like the defendant's agreement to testify for the government in another case. Usually the prosecutor's only gain is a reduction of the number of cases for trial, about which he can be flexible at any particular time. He negotiates pleas simply because that is how the process works. Since the original charges do not reflect anyone's careful decision that a conviction on those charges would be proper, he does not start with the attitude that the defendant's conviction of anything less is a sacrifice. Although simply as a matter of professional competence he would try to prove at trial the most serious charges that the evidence will support, all he needs in order to accept a plea of guilty to less serious charges is a general sense that justice will be as well served that way. The uncertainties of sentencing and the leveling of variations in sentence by prison and parole practices make it easy for him to be satisfied. He is not likely to have much confidence in imprisonment except as a means of "putting away" the defendant for a while. Much as the police having cleared a crime are not directly concerned with the subsequent prosecution, once the prosecutor has secured an appropriate conviction he is not much concerned with its consequences; he probably deplores our penal practices without feeling that his own professional responsibilities are implicated.

The defendant, of course, is presumed to plead guilty and give up his chance for an acquittal at trial mainly in order to reduce his punishment. Occasionally, the reduction is certain and substantial; sometimes, for example, by pleading guilty to a lesser offense he can avoid conviction of a crime for which an unusually severe sentence is mandatory. Usually, the hoped-for reduction is dependent on the exercise of discretion by the sentencing judge; but since it may be substantial, and in comparison with the possible sentence for the original charges almost always is substantial, it is attractive even though uncertain. More often than the prevalence of guilty pleas suggests, the concrete benefit to the defendant is small or even imaginary. The practice of imposing concurrent sentences for more than one crime, the broad range of sentencing alternatives for most crimes, and the inclusion of the facts of the crime in the judge's presentence report all make it less important whether some charges are dismissed or for which of related crimes the sentence is imposed. If there is a substantial sentencing advantage, its impact on the actual term of imprisonment often is much less because of provisions for "good time" credit and parole and because the defendant commonly has "backup time" to serve from a previous conviction.* Since the decision to plead normally is made without certainty about what sentence will be imposed, defendants rationally plead guilty in the hope of obtaining a benefit. And since the sentence is less than the maximum possible sentence, a defendant can rarely be sure that he did not obtain some benefit.†

The charges to which the defendant pleads guilty are arranged in a brief conversation between the two lawyers. They may have a meeting in the prosecutor's office or talk in a hallway of the courthouse or a courtroom where both happen to be present for another purpose or on the telephone. There is nothing novel about most negotiations, and the result is predictable. Neither lawyer bases his "bargaining position" on a detailed examination of the particular facts of the case. For many crimes there is a standard lesser offense to which the defendant is ordinarily expected to plead. If he is charged with a number of similar crimes or several crimes arising out of one incident, the one to which he will plead and the ones which will be dismissed are determined quickly and routinely. Even in special circumstances when the case or the defendant is out of the ordinary, the plea is worked out according to a more or less

*"Backup time" is the unexpired portion of a previous sentence which has to be served if a person released on parole violates the conditions of parole; a conviction of another crime while still on parole is usually an automatic violation. If the series of sentences is very long, the time when parole is granted may be affected little by their precise total.

†Recommendations that the uncertainty be eliminated by judicial supervision of plea bargains or the judge's announcement of what sentence he intends to impose before a plea becomes final have not been widely adopted, perhaps because they resemble too much the King's suggestion to Alice that there be "sentence first, trial afterwards." One consequence of such a procedure would be to make it much harder to justify imposition of a more severe sentence after trial if the defendant decided to go to trial after a plea had been worked out.

understood formula. In the language of economics, the plea resembles a "normal price" much more than a juncture of "marginal utilities."

There are exceptions. In a highly publicized case, the prosecutor may feel pressure to display a particularly firm or, more rarely, gentle hand. A defense counsel who has been retained at a large fee and is expected to perform accordingly may be unable to recommend to his client any plea within the range of those that the prosecutor will accept. In an ordinary case, an unusually conscientious defense counsel may work hard to show that his client is special; he may, for example, help the defendant to get a job and then try to arrange a plea that will lead to a suspended sentence and probation on the ground that the defendant is (at least or at last) working and should be given a chance.

The prosecutor and defense counsel work out a bargain because they have a common understanding that a bargain will be worked out. The prosecutor does not speak to the defendant. He does not want to speak to him, and even if he did it would be improper to do so. By the time the trial date approaches, the defendant understands that a trial is not to be expected. He is not likely to resist the proposed plea if his lawyer tells him that he cannot do better, which is what defense counsel, believing that he has done his job satisfactorily, tells him. If the defendant does turn down the proposal, defense counsel may return to the prosecutor; but the bargain is not likely to change. They both know that having asserted himself, the defendant probably will accept the plea in the end.

The actual plea of guilty is a perfunctory exercise in which formalities triumph over substance. The defendant is required to respond to a catechism designed to ensure that his decision to forgo a trial is voluntary and that he understands its consequences. He is asked if he is pleading guilty "because he is guilty and for no other reason," and if any threats or promises were made to him to induce the plea. While some judges require the prosecutor or the defendant himself to describe the crime, little if any effort is made to prove the defendant's guilt beyond his plea. The Supreme Court, indeed, has declared that it is not constitutionally improper to accept a guilty plea from (and to convict and punish) a person who at the same time protests his innocence of the crime.[2]

The questions put to a defendant and his answers insulate the conviction from later attack on the ground that he did not know what he was doing. But they add nothing to the substance of the plea and ought not to increase our confidence in it. The plea is explicitly the product of a bargain in which each party is acting for his own benefit. If in some special sense it can be said that the state is acting also for the defendant's benefit, which is doubtful, the defendant is certainly not acting in any interest except his own. Having decided that it is in his best interest to plead guilty, the proceeding is for him merely a ritual. So far as *his* interest is concerned, nothing turns on the accuracy of his answers; all that counts is that the answers be "right," so that the plea will be accepted. The result too often is a proceeding that is transparently staged. The judge may leave the questioning to his clerk, who asks the defendant questions in a swift monotone. The defendant answers mechanically, perhaps saying "Yes" when he should say "No" ("Have any promises been made to you?") or the reverse ("Are you pleading guilty because you are guilty and for no other reason?") until his lawyer nudges him in the ribs and he corrects himself.

One of the dilemmas that confronts defense counsel is that he must instruct his client how to answer questions about the crime in such a way that the plea will be accepted.

If the defendant has not unequivocally admitted facts constituting the crime or has denied facts essential to the crime,
should defense counsel instruct him to answer differently if
the judge insists on an admission of the offense along with
the plea? Various courts have expressed outrage at the idea
that defense counsel should coach his client to appear guilty
lest the plea not be accepted. But in view of the system's
own willingness to disregard proof of guilt, what else can be
expected? In practice, here as elsewhere, lawyers commonly
find some verbal formula that throws a cloak of ambiguity
over their duty to apply mutually inconsistent principles.

The assertion that a plea of guilty is the defendant's
independent choice is valuable to us because it protects the
myth of an adversary trial process, which does not survive
frank recognition that most of the time the only "defense"
is a quick, informal exchange between the prosecutor and
defense counsel. To say that the defendant chooses to forgo
the trial that would normally be his and the prosecutor,
honoring the defendant's responsible freedom, accepts his
choice is comforting but false.

The most important national legal bodies, including the
Supreme Court and the American Bar Association, have
endorsed the negotiation of guilty pleas as part of the normal
criminal process.[3] The grounds of their endorsement betray
a chilling remoteness from the realities of criminal justice
and indicate the ideological importance of the prevailing
"trial" model. The institutionalized practices by which pleas
of guilty are arranged and accepted corrupt criminal justice.

The usual justification for plea bargaining has two
components. The first, in the language of the Supreme
Court, is that the defendant "demonstrates by his plea that
he is ready and willing to admit his crime and to enter the

correctional system in a frame of mind that affords hope for success in rehabilitation over a shorter period of time than might otherwise be necessary.''[4] The defendant's acknowledgement of his wrongdoing, it is asserted, is a step on the path to rectitude. Awareness of one's wrongdoing and willingness to accept responsibility for it are, it is true, widely believed to tend toward good behavior. But application of that generalization to a plea of guilty before trial can be described only as wildly improbable. No serious person who knows how an ordinary plea agreement is reached or has observed the procedure for entry of a plea in court could believe that the fact that a defendant has pleaded guilty has any bearing on the likelihood of his rehabilitation. There is certainly no evidence that that is so. The defendant's willingness to submit to judgment is not the product of an impulse to mend his ways; it is based on a calculation that by doing so he will reduce his punishment. Many persons would regard it as an imposition on the defendant to insist that he be contrite (or more realistically, that he act as if he were) when he pleads guilty. Contrition is beside the point. Defendants plead guilty long after the commission of a crime, usually on the eve of a trial. If it is sensible to speculate at all, one might as easily speculate that a trial at which the defendant is obliged to confront his victim offers the more promising prospect for rehabilitation.

The argument that by pleading guilty the defendant gives a sign that he has reformed is evidently embarrassing to those who make it. It is buttressed by the argument that whatever may be his state of mind, the defendant has helped the state to accomplish its purpose. The American Bar Association, for example, has said that one reason for granting a sentencing concession is ''that the defendant by his plea has aided in ensuring the prompt and certain application of correctional measures to him,'' and ''that the concessions will make possible alternative correctional measures which are better adapted to achieving rehabilitative, protective, deterrent or other purposes of correctional treatment, or will prevent undue harm to the defendant from the form of conviction.''[5] Since a defendant rarely pleads guilty before the trial is imminent and his plea normally is followed by further delay while the judge considers his sentence, so far as this argument depends on ''the *prompt* . . . application of correctional measures,'' it is generally false. With respect to the selection of ''alternative correctional measures,'' it is never the case that a defendant pleads guilty in order to obtain a *more* severe sentence. The argument depends, therefore, on the assumption that by going to trial a defendant might subject himself to a punishment that is too severe and serves both himself and the state less well than some milder punishment might. But a sentencing disposition favorable to the defendant does not need to depend on his willingness not to be tried. A judge can impose the lighter sentence just as easily if the defendant is convicted after a trial as if he pleads guilty.* All that is left of the argument is that plea bargaining allows us to convict and sentence an undetermined number of persons who would not be convicted at a trial: ''the . . . *certain* application of correctional measures.'' If that proposition means anything concrete at all, it means that we use the pressure of plea bargaining to convict defendants whose guilt we might not be able to establish at a trial. Whatever merit there may be in such an argument obviously depends at least on the assumption that the pressure is not so great that persons who are in

*It is true that in some, albeit not very many, cases conviction on the original charge would require an unduly harsh sentence. But it is not necessary that the defendant plead guilty to avoid such a result; if conviction on the original charge would not be appropriate, the prosecutor can reduce the charge accordingly without insisting that the defendant give up a trial.

fact innocent yield to it and plead guilty.* If that assumption is sound and is sufficient to overcome all the values of a trial, then the trial system itself as a general method of establishing guilt is called into question.

The other component of the justification for plea bargaining goes to the heart of the matter. The bargain is recognized explicitly as a transaction in which unrelated objectives of the defendant and the state are served. The defendant wants to minimize his punishment, wholly without regard to its possible benefit to society or himself. The state wants to avoid a trial. By forbearing to punish the defendant as much as he deserves, the state serves other social ends. More particularly, the argument is that the survival of adversary trials in present conditions depends on there not being too many of them. We can offer a trial to all only if few accept the offer. The practice of plea bargaining has this effect, so that whatever the defects of the practice itself the criminal process as a whole is the better for it. Plea bargaining conserves "scarce judicial and prosecutorial resources. . . for those cases in which there is a substantial issue of the defendant's guilt or in which there is substantial doubt that the State can sustain its burden of proof."[6] It is not an offense to justice if a guilty person exchanges his right to a trial for a sentencing concession, the argument concludes, because his plea does not make him worse off; and at least some of the persons who plead guilty are better off than they would have been had they been convicted after a trial.†

*The Supreme Court has said: "We would have serious doubts about . . . [plea bargaining] if the encouragement of guilty pleas by offers of leniency substantially increased the likelihood that defendants, advised by competent counsel, would falsely condemn themselves. But our view is to the contrary. . . . " Brady v. United States, 397 U.S. 742, 758 (1970).

†Some persons who plead guilty would not have been found guilty at a trial. But, it is assumed, they are guilty and should in that sense have

This argument ignores the defendants who do *not* plead guilty, go to trial, and are convicted. More generally, by focusing on the advantage to the defendant in some cases, it ignores the significance for the criminal process of "bargain" justice. If it is true that those who plead guilty receive a sentencing concession, it is true that those who go to trial and are convicted are denied a sentencing concession that they might have had. The loss of the benefit obtained by those who plead guilty is in its effect a penalty imposed on those who are convicted following a trial.

Consider a concrete case. The defendant has broken into a shop, stolen articles of small value, and made off in a car taken from the street. He is accused of breaking and entering, petty larceny, and unauthorized use of a motor vehicle. The prosecutor and defense counsel agree that he will plead guilty to the last charge, which carries a maximum sentence of imprisonment for five years and a likely sentence of one to five years, which will probably mean imprisonment for eighteen months followed by parole. After discussing the proposal with defense counsel, the defendant decides to go to trial. He is convicted on all three counts, the first of which carries a maximum sentence of imprisonment for fifteen years (and the second a maximum sentence of one year). On what justifiable basis can his sentence be greater than it would have been had he pleaded guilty as arranged? If it is greater, is there any way to argue that he has not paid a price for going to trial?*

It is not beyond possibility that one would respond to these rhetorical questions thus: "Yes, it is true that a

---

been convicted; and had they been convicted after a trial, their sentence would not have been less.

*Perhaps it can be asserted meaningfully that the severity of his sentence is a consequence of his decision but not caused by it; either way, the extra penalty is the price of the decision.

defendant who goes to trial and is convicted pays a price. We make a trial costly because we cannot afford to have a trial for everyone and it is very important that we have a trial for some: those who are innocent and will be acquitted. Since they are not sentenced at all, they lose nothing by having gone to trial. Not knowing who they are until after the trial, we make the decision to go to trial costly in a way that will reduce the number of guilty defendants who demand a trial to a manageable level without reducing the number of innocent defendants who demand a trial. We accomplish that by imposing a cost only on persons who are found guilty after trial.''*

If it were true that we could not be assured of acquitting the innocent without a trial and that we could not afford a trial in every case, it is plausible that we should elect to punish unduly those who are found guilty after trial rather than risk punishing the innocent at all. But we ought not to accept easily the conclusion that the only reliable method of determining guilt is so far beyond our resources that we need immediately to find ways to avoid using it very much even if that means punishing some persons excessively. If that were our conclusion, we should have to reconsider whether it would not be better sometimes to forgo convicting the guilty. And, of course, we could no longer describe our criminal process as based on an ''adversary'' or ''trial'' system.

*One might ask why, if the cost is explicitly functional and not based on desert, it should be assessed by extra imprisonment, which itself uses up society's resources, and not be convertible as most things are into a dollar value. Why must the wealthy guilty man pay for his trial by extra imprisonment instead of being assessed the full cost of the trial? Since the cost would be assessed only against those who were convicted, a poor man who was innocent would not be denied justice. That is a question that someone who made the argument explicitly might not be able to answer. One answer, perhaps the only one, would be simply that the polity demands that certain appearances be preserved.

The argument that those who are convicted after a trial should pay a price for it has not been accepted. Just the opposite. A trial judge's frank statement after a trial that if the defendant had pleaded guilty he would have received a lighter sentence has been flatly and forcefully disapproved.[7] The American Bar Association has declared: "The court should not impose upon a defendant any sentence in excess of that which would be justified by any of the rehabilitative, protective, deterrent or other purposes of the criminal law because the defendant has chosen to require the prosecution to prove his guilt at trial rather than to enter a plea of guilty. . . ."[8] It is certain that explicit adoption of a rule which imposed, say, a surcharge of 10 percent of one's punishment on persons convicted after trial would be unconstitutional. Yet it is simply schizophrenic to assert that although a concession is granted for pleading guilty, a penalty is not exacted for not pleading guilty.[9] We do, it is true, distinguish between giving a reward for service and exacting a penalty for disservice. In this context, however, since a guilty plea is the normal course, in ordinary usage the situation would be described as one involving a penalty imposed on those who go to trial.*

While the range and extent of punishment as a response to crime depend generally on a society's resources and their allocation, it is another matter altogether that the punishment in particular cases should vary according to the cost of

---

*One judge who, unlike most of his judicial brothers, has faced the problem has acknowledged that a price is paid for going to trial. His explanation is that when the defendant elects to go to trial he gambles for an acquittal. The extra severity of his sentence if he is convicted is the price he pays for the gamble, which the man who pleads guilty doesn't have. Scott v. United States, 419 F.2d 264, 276–77 (D.C. Cir. 1969) (Bazelon, J.). While one must give candor its due, especially when it is so rare, the justification that is offered is stunning. What does the notion of gambling have to do with the imposition of punishment for wrongdoing?

proving the defendant's guilt. There may be a utilitarian justification for a differential of that kind; but it would require us to accept explicitly the practice of imposing undeserved punishment as the price of whatever social benefit was obtained, and we have not—at least in principle—done so. Even if we were able somehow to accept punishing a defendant more severely because he insisted that we prove that he deserved to be punished at all, our normal reliance on a bargain for the critical determination of guilt undermines fundamentally the notion of criminal justice. The negotiated exchange of benefits has nothing to do with the claim that punishment is deserved. If the punishment imposed is usually a "normal price" for the crime and the defendant's benefit from his bargain is less than he hoped, nevertheless he is institutionally encouraged to believe that he is trading some of his freedom in order not to be deprived of more. If his freedom is so readily negotiated, with so little concern for what punishment he actually deserves, he will not easily understand the justification for punishing him at all.

Having only the defendant's calculation of his own advantage and lacking any careful determination of what he has actually done, we can have no assurance that like acts are punished alike. The assumption of the Supreme Court and others that "the innocent" do not plead guilty treats criminal guilt too much as if it were unequivocal and entirely independent of the process by which guilt is established. If we can be sure that persons who are unequivocally innocent do not plead guilty, we can be sure also that plea bargaining does not resolve uniformly the details and ambiguities on which an accurate determination of guilt and desert to be punished depend.

5

TRIAL

The rhetoric of American criminal justice gives the trial in court unique value. Everything that precedes it is conceived as preparation; what follows is aftermath. A trial is the most visible and dramatic event in the criminal process, the most formal and sustained display of the majesty and authority of the law. When the government prosecutes, so we are to understand, it solemnly intends to bring the case to court, which regrettably but for sufficient reasons often does not occur because the defendant chooses to plead guilty. That description plainly has little to do with the facts. Even if it were true that the manner in which we conduct a trial had the virtues claimed for it, it would be doubtful that we should sacrifice as much as we do in most cases to have those virtues in a few. But the objections to our trial procedures are much stronger than that. On their own terms, even if they did not impose unreasonable

87

demands on the system as a whole, the most distinctive features of a criminal trial in this country should not be regarded as virtues. They are generally contrary to any of the purposes for which the trial is supposed to be conducted.

THE JURY

Service on a jury has traditionally been regarded as part privilege and part civic duty, for which either way little compensation need be paid. Since a person summoned for jury duty may have to serve for a period of weeks or several months, it is something that most people are glad to avoid, privilege or not. Jury lists contain the names of the competent adult population of the community. But courts are understandably reluctant to require service of persons who cannot easily adjust their normal commitments to a schedule that may keep them in court for six or more hours a day. Virtually all professional people and most people who have regular jobs or have to care for children at home are ordinarily excused from service. Almost any other claim of hardship other than simply the hardship of the largely unremunerated task of being a juror is likely to be accepted as an excuse. Juries tend, therefore, to be composed of persons who are less regularly and actively engaged in daily affairs than most adults; a disproportionate number are retired men and women who do not have regular duties at home. From an economic point of view, that is as it should be; jury service usefully and a little bit gainfully employs persons who are willing and not busy elsewhere.

So long as the civic virtue of serving on a jury must be its only significant reward, a liberal policy of exemption for hardship is practically unavoidable. It does, however, produce a population of jurors systematically different from the general population in ways that look as though they must affect the outcome of some criminal trials. Most of us would expect middle-aged women and somewhat older men drawn mostly from the lower and middle ranges of the middle economic class to have attitudes about many crimes that can be differentiated from attitudes of some other groups in the population. It is certain that a statute which explicitly limited jurors to such persons would be summarily rejected. The fact that we accept the same result by indirection suggests that our incredible emphasis on the selection of particular jurors after the jury pool has been chosen is inflated and has another explanation than actual differences among the jurors.

Persons who have been summoned for jury duty wait in the jurors' "lounge" until they are called for a trial. It is usually a depressing place, partly because it is badly equipped but more because time is so palpably being wasted; jurors drink coffee, read old magazines, play cards, and wait. At the beginning of a trial, a panel of jurors is summoned to the courtroom. The trial judge (or his clerk) asks for a panel large enough in his estimation to yield a jury of twelve after all eliminations. Thirty jurors are probably enough in an ordinary case; in special, celebrated cases, hundreds of jurors may be examined before twelve are accepted.

The examination and selection of a jury, known as the *voir dire,* begins the trial; it may take as much time as the presentation of evidence. In its first stage, the prospective jurors are asked obvious questions about their knowledge of the case and acquaintance with the defendant or any of the principal figures in the trial that might color their view of the evidence. Unless the community is so small or the crime so notorious that entirely uninformed, neutral jurors cannot be found, any significant prior knowledge of the case or the people involved is a basis for excusing a juror. Usually this part of the *voir dire* takes just a few minutes.

In a seriously contested case, there are additional

questions. Defense counsel commonly asks the jurors about their attitudes toward the police and the victims of crime:

1. Does the juror have relatives who are policemen or work in law enforcement?
2. If the prosecutor should call a policeman as a witness, would the juror give his testimony undue weight just because he is a police officer?
3. Has the juror or anyone close to him been the victim of a crime like the one charged against the defendant?

If there is an issue of the defendant's mental competence, both the prosecutor and defense counsel may inquire extensively into jurors' attitudes toward psychiatrists (who will be called as expert witnesses on the issue) and beliefs about free will. If the defendant or the victim was a member of an identifiable minority group, there may be questions designed to reveal prejudice against that group. When bias because of a common but infrequently avowed prejudice is feared, defense counsel or less often the prosecutor may want not only to ask about it directly but also to ask for information like social affiliations that might suggest prejudice.

The scope and duration of such questioning vary. While the trial judge generally has authority to limit questions as he believes appropriate, he and the lawyers work within an understood range of permissible inquiry. If a lawyer (usually defense counsel) wants to question extensively, it takes a long time. Answers that have any likelihood of significance are followed by further questions probing the details of the initial response. In an occasional spectacular case, in which each prospective juror is examined individually and at length and many are excused, the *voir dire* may continue for weeks. Most of the time, a jury is selected within an hour or less if the case is uncomplicated and within several hours if there is a special issue like insanity to consider.

A juror whose answers reveal a solid basis for doubting his ability to consider the case objectively is excused "for cause." In a routine case, aside from their prior knowledge about it and relationships to the persons involved, jurors' answers to questions do not often require that they be excused for cause. But if one side or the other challenges a juror, it is often easier for the judge and more efficient to excuse the juror and send him back to the jury room than to examine the claim of bias closely (and, if it is the defense that makes the challenge, risk an appeal from its denial if the defendant is convicted). While the practice of allowing extended questioning itself lends credence to claims that the answers are significant, in the important affairs of daily life we do not assume that almost any prior experience related to the matter at hand disqualifies a person from forming a judgment about it. Our usual assumption is that at least on matters not affecting themselves, for all their special attitudes and experiences people nevertheless make reasonable judgments.

If the only purpose of extending the *voir dire* beyond the standard initial questions were to exclude jurors whose objectivity was doubtful, extended questioning often would demonstrably be a waste of time. The main reason why the lawyers engage in it is just the reverse: to include on the jury, if they can, persons who are likely to be favorably disposed to their side of the case. Each side is allowed a number of "peremptory challenges," which eliminate jurors without any inquiry into the reasons for the challenge. Usually they are based on membership in some group: the old, the young, women, men, blacks, whites, homeowners, union members, civil rights workers. They may be based on an actual or fancied resistance to the lawyer when the juror answered his questions, or on the juror's face. They are, simply, peremptory.*

Since such challenges do not need to be based on generally accepted grounds for suspecting partiality, they greatly enlarge the potential scope of questioning; restriction of almost any line of questions may deny the questioner an opportunity to uncover a fact that he deems significant even if no one else does. The prosecutor rarely pursues such questioning very far; in that respect as in others he is part of a team to which the judge also belongs. When defense counsel wants to question extensively, his questions are limited by a combination of mutual forbearance and a tug-of-war between him and the judge. His questions must appear to be related to some suspicion of prejudice, well founded or not, with which the judge is not wholly unfamiliar. In order not to probe too much into a juror's personal affairs, defense counsel may ask him questions intended to indicate indirectly his religion, politics, or economic circumstances, from which, on the basis of popular conceptions, he guesses the juror's attitudes about the issues which will be important at trial. He may also guess a juror's background from his surname or his address and occupation, which are often given on the jury list.

*The procedure for exercising peremptory challenges varies and sometimes allows considerable gamesmanship. According to a report in *The New York Times* of a seminar on trial tactics, one of the instructors, who was a prominent prosecutor, described the following as one of his "favorite tricks": "When questioning prospective jurors, he often has an associate in the courtroom who gives a slight nod if the juror is acceptable. After his opponent has noticed the signals . . . the associate might shake his head negatively at a juror the defense ordinarily would challenge. The defense lawyer, assuming [the prosecutor] will challenge the juror, does not exercise his own challenge and is dismayed to find an unwelcome member seated on the jury." *The New York Times*, September 22, 1973, p.33. The trick may be a favorite, but one supposes that occasions for its use are rare.

One reputable trial manual generally approves as good jurors for the defendant "salesmen, actors, artists and writers" who "have enjoyed wide and varied experiences, have witnessed the good and bad in people and are prone to forgive an indiscretion in another"; undesirable jurors include "retired police officers, military men and their wives" and "bankers, bank employees, members of management, and low-salaried white-collar workers."[1] Another teaches that least likely to be receptive to the defense of insanity "would be the Roman Catholic with his emphasis upon free will, moral responsibility and payment for sins"; most likely, Unitarians, Jews, Congregationalists, and Presbyterians. Jurors from the "urban North" are more receptive to the insanity defense than those from the "rural South or the farming Mid-West." Those with Scandinavian backgrounds are more receptive than "the sentimental Irish and sympathetic Italian," and so forth.[2]

No other country has a procedure remotely similar to the *voir dire* as it is practiced here. Its main justification is said to be that in a heterogeneous society only the allowance of challenges without any explanation assures a defendant a jury of *his* peers. That justification plainly is irrelevant to peremptory challenges by the prosecution.* As for the defendant, he almost never has anything to do with the questions or the challenges, which express his lawyer's intuitions (and biases) rather than his own. Were he to intervene in the *voir dire*, even by whispering to his lawyer, he would be told to rely on the latter's judgment, as he should if the lawyer has the professional skill for which he is

*In ordinary cases, prosecutors generally exercise their right to challenge peremptorily less than do defense counsel. Under the "struck juror" system, by which each side in turn eliminates one member of the panel (after all excuses for cause have been made) until twelve remain, the prosecutor cannot avoid making peremptory choices unless he devises a mechanical or random formula for his strikes.

paid. The defendant does not care how well he "relates" to the jurors; he cares about the verdict, with respect to which the lawyer's hunches are the best he has to go on. It is true that many defendants do not perceive the societal group from which the jurors are selected as a group to which they also belong. That problem is not alleviated at all by peremptory challenges. Indeed, the prosecutor's or even defense counsel's challenges may deny the defendant representation on the jury of members of a group with which he does identify. Lawyers sometimes assert that if they could not exercise peremptory challenges, their questions to elicit actual bias would have to be limited lest they antagonize a juror who could not then be removed. Questions that are seriously framed to reveal bias can be asked by the judge, a suggestion which lawyers strenuously resist. Whoever asks the questions, were a juror to display actual antagonism to either side, that would be a basis for his removal for cause.

From the point of view of a defense counsel or prosecutor, peremptory challenges are a straightforward attempt to affect the outcome of a trial. The literature of trial tactics is full of advice about how to identify favorable and unfavorable jurors, not only from information that they give but also from their appearance and mannerisms.* Notwithstanding the advice, the most that the lawyers can do is rely on their rational or irrational hunches about persons concerning whom, even after extensive questioning, they know almost nothing. There is little reason to believe that in most cases a

*For example: "Generally speaking, the heavy, roundfaced, jovial-looking person is the most desirable [for the defense]. The undesirable juror is quite often the slight, underweight and delicate type. His features are sharp and fragile, with that lean 'Cassius' look. The athletic-looking juror is hard to categorize. Usually he is hard to convince; but once convinced he will usually go all the way for you." F. Lee Bailey and Henry B. Rothblatt, Fundamentals of Criminal Advocacy 284–85 (1974).

jury selected after an intensive *voir dire* is predictably "better" from any point of view than a group of twelve competent jurors selected at random. The lawyer's information about each juror is too little, the factors determining jurors' votes are too many and too uncertain, the extent and manner of each juror's participation in the jury's deliberations and verdict are too unpredictable for reliable guesses about how each of them will react to evidence he has not yet heard.

Lawyers who secure favorable verdicts understandably pounce on every *post facto* indication that this or that juror, who the lawyer thought was "with him," held out for his side. Understandably, they do not make much of unfavorable verdicts. Understandably also, the jurors who are willing to speak to a lawyer after a verdict are those most likely to feed his hope that his ability and performance had something to do with the favorable result. Since the purpose of peremptory challenges is to affect the verdict, the assertion after a favorable verdict that the lawyer did his work successfully cannot be disproved; it is easy enough *post hoc* to assert *propter hoc*. Sometimes, albeit rarely, it is clear that a particular person's presence on the jury was highly significant, especially because verdicts need to be unanimous. In that sense, the procedure of selection which kept a dissenting juror on the jury but might have excluded him was important to the result. It is tempting but misleading to conclude in such cases that the winning lawyer's ability to "size up" jurors was a critical factor in the trial. We have no way to tell whether such cases occur more often or predictably than they would were there no peremptory challenges at all.

A defense counsel who conducts a prolonged *voir dire* cannot be faulted. In the context of an adversary process in which he is to do "his utmost" for his client, giving him the opportunity to choose among prospective jurors is not much different from obliging him to do so. Having the opportunity, he properly learns as much as he can and then uses whatever information he has to make his best guess. If the guess is not likely to be any worse, a small chance that it may be better is worth taking. Even if a lawyer were inclined privately to dismiss peremptory challenges as a waste of time, therefore, it is difficult for him to do so if they are used extensively by others and his client and professional peers are watching his performance.

Lawyers sometimes assert that the oral examination of jurors is itself useful even if the challenges that result are not. The *voir dire* is the only occasion during the trial, so the argument goes, when a lawyer can have a conversation with individual jurors. Trial manuals tell how to prepare a jury for the theory of the defense. Defense counsel may ask prospective jurors whether they can give someone accused of a crime the benefit of a doubt, as the standard of "proof beyond a reasonable doubt" requires; the jurors having affirmed (usually by their silence) that they can, in his closing argument he reminds them of their "promise" and tries to "cash it in." Excellent trial lawyers say that such tactics make a great difference. But it is difficult to believe that in so highly structured a proceeding, jurors are so motivated by first, fleeting impressions of the lawyers that their votes are affected. It is not surprising that lawyers insist on the importance of forensic virtuosity. The *voir dire* is an opportunity for them to play a large role in the trial, to convince their clients (and themselves) that they are working and by affecting the very composition of the jury getting results. How could counsel, performing under the watchful eyes of the defendant, not make as much as he can of such an opportunity? Lawyers should not be criticized for behaving like lawyers.

If the lawyers' examination and selection of jurors does predictably affect the outcome of trials in a significant number of cases, as those who defend our current practices assert, that is the strongest reason not to allow it. It is one thing for lawyers to favor a practice by which they can influence the outcome of a trial. But, beyond the elimination of persons whose bias prevents them from judging fairly, what societal objective is served by letting the determination of a defendant's guilt or innocence depend *at all* on a lawyer's ability to guess jurors' attitudes or to establish a relationship with them? Of what relevance to the functions of the trial is his ability to make shrewd guesses about how this or that juror's personal characteristics will affect his reaction to the evidence?

Whether one accepts the claims for the *voir dire* or believes, as I do, that they are greatly exaggerated, it should be cut down. At best it is a waste of time. At worst it makes the determination of a person's guilt depend in appearance and in fact on irrelevancies. In the very selection of the persons who will decide whether the defendant is guilty, the *voir dire* introduces an explicitly tactical factor wholly unrelated to guilt. Were the *voir dire* strictly confined to its purpose, the composition of a fair, reliable jury, and all techniques intended to prejudice the selection favorably to one side or the other eliminated, the entire process of selecting jurors could be accomplished within a few minutes.

PROVING THE CASE

Once a jury has been sworn and installed in the jury box, the format of a trial based on the adversary relationship between prosecution and defense is familiar. The two sides present and argue their cases in an alternating pattern that gives the trial rhythm and symmetry. The prosecutor, who has the burden of proof, goes first. He summarizes the government's evidence in an opening statement and then presents his witnesses in whatever order he chooses. Defense counsel follows with his witnesses.* Thereafter each side is allowed to call additional witnesses to testify only about issues raised in the preceding testimony of the opposing side. When there are no further witnesses, the two lawyers make closing arguments to the jury, the prosecutor typically being given both the first and last word. The same alternating rhythm is repeated within the case for each side. After a witness has given "direct" testimony for the side that has called him as a witness, he is "cross" examined by the opposing lawyer. He may then be examined on "redirect," "recross," and so forth, limited each time to the issues elicited in his testimony immediately before. The original cross-examination and all succeeding questions are, therefore, limited to the issues raised in a witness's direct testimony; if the opposing lawyer wants his testimony on other isues, he has to call him as "his own" witness.

These large and small patterns of alternation and opposition illustrate the most important features of an American criminal trial: its complete bifurcation into two separate "cases" and the control of the proof by the prosecutor and defense counsel. There are elaborate theories of justification for both. But even at their most extravagant the justifications do not reach the concrete consequences of practices which, but for their familiarity, we should regard as peculiar in the extreme. The conduct of a criminal trial resembles a highly ritualized struggle between good and evil, the State

---

*The opening statement for the defense may be made immediately after the prosecutor's statement, before any evidence is presented, or after the prosecution is complete, just before presentation of the evidence for the defense.

and the Malefactor, more than it does an effort to determine facts. In that respect, it retains scarcely below the surface traces of the ancient trial by combat.

The bifurcation of a trial into the "prosecution" and the "defense" allows for no undistributed middle. Unless one lawyer or the other perceives an advantage from a witness's testimony within the framework of the case the lawyer will present, the witness will not testify at all. Even if he has information that would be helpful to a disinterested investigator, he may not be called to testify if the information is ambiguous, if he knows something else that the lawyer whom the information helps wants to keep concealed, if in the lawyer's opinion he will not make a good impression on the jury, or if for any reason his testimony will not predictably be helpful to one side or the other.

The consequences of bifurcation are not only that occasionally witnesses who could aid the factfinding process are not heard. More generally, the testimony of a witness is shaped and packaged to meet the particular needs of the side for which he testifies, according to the general assumption that all testimony favors one side or the other. The more simple, direct, and—above all—unequivocal a witness's testimony is, the "better" it is, although just those qualities perhaps would ordinarily make it suspect. Jurors identify witnesses with the prosecution or defense, which gets the benefit (or harm) of the identifications. Witnesses identify themselves similarly so that they resist giving information that may aid "the other side."

The responsibility of the prosecutor and defense counsel is to present the evidence favorable to their respective sides in the strongest light. Which witnesses are summoned, the order in which they testify, and what questions they are asked are all matters governed exclusively by the lawyer's unconstrained strategy for supporting one side of the case.

The prosecutor has a duty to inform defense counsel and perhaps the court of evidence favorable to the defense if he has reason to suppose that the counsel does not know about it. He has no duty to put the evidence before the jury. If for some reason defense counsel failed to present the evidence, the prosecutor could not do so himself without antagonizing his opponent and convincing the jurors that he wanted them to acquit the defendant. Defense counsel's role is clearer. It would be a violation of his professional responsibility even to advise the prosecutor of evidence against the defendant's interest. Were he deliberately to call as a witness a person whose testimony was unfavorable to the defendant, that would be a sufficient basis for concluding that he was incompetent and that the defendant was denied his right to the effective assistance of counsel.

Before the trial, a careful prosecutor or defense counsel helps his witnesses to bring uncertain recollections into focus. He encourages them to give firm answers to questions that they would not even have formulated without his tutelage, so that their perception of the critical facts appears sharper and more certain than it was. He helps them to be calm and credible witnesses, whose testimony is convincing. He discusses with them what questions he will ask and what the answers will be, what questions to anticipate on cross-examination, what "traps" opposing counsel may spring and how to avoid them. If there is need, he tells them how to dress.

If one witness tells the prosecutor that the criminal was about five feet tall and was wearing a gray overcoat and another witness tells him that the criminal was six feet tall and wearing a tan raincoat, it is proper and professionally competent for him to try to resolve the disagreement before the trial. So long as he acts with restraint, he can ask a witness to reconsider his own recollections in light of the inconsistent recollections of another witness, as a way genuinely to resolve a disputed matter of fact. His task is to present a "case" for the defendant's guilt, not an unintegrated mess of relevant data. But however carefully he avoids explicit pressure to reach an agreement and suggests to witnesses that they "just think about it some more," at the trial the witnesses' recollections of detail are likely to be less uncertain and more uniform that they were. If, as we must hope, such "cleaning up" of the evidence does not often distort witnesses' testimony about a "simple" fact like the identification of a criminal, it is likely to affect the jury's impressions of more complicated fact patterns on which critical issues of guilt may depend. After preparing a witness, the lawyer may admonish him, "Remember, just tell the truth." Lest the message be lost, he may add, "If the defense counsel [or prosecutor] asks you on the stand whether you discussed this case with me, say that you did and that I told you just to tell the truth."

During the trial, questions are phrased to elicit only that bit of information that will be favorable. If the witness has been prepared well, his direct testimony is straightforward, since the questions and answers have been worked out ahead of time. On cross-examination, a witness may not accept so easily the opposing lawyer's effort to shape his testimony. A witness who has a larger sense of his own responsibility for what he says or who resists being made to serve an opposed cause is told in the time-worn phrase, "Just answer the question." If he persists in expanding his answers beyond the precise questions asked, the lawyer will ask the judge to admonish the witness, which the judge will do.

Having available a witness who is honest and certain about an important piece of evidence, counsel's suspicion that the witness may be mistaken bears primarily on the question "Will he stand up under cross-examination?" Even if his suspicion of mistake is strong, the prosecutor probably will "let the jury decide" unless tactical considerations dictate that he not call the witness. Were defense counsel not to present a witness who he thought was honest solely because he thought the witness was in fact mistaken, it would be a failure of his duty to the defendant. Similarly, cross-examination of a witness is independent of any view about the accuracy of his testimony. So far as he can, counsel "shakes" an opposing witness's testimony by revealing if not indeed creating minor inconsistencies, insisting on precision about trivia and then either lamenting the imprecision or pouncing on another inconsistency, and making the witness behave nervously or otherwise look unreliable.

In one way or another, every aspect of the trial is distorted by the presentation of evidence exclusively through the prisms of the prosecution and defense. The substitution of tactics for principle pervades the trial. In one of the few cases to deal with the issue explicitly, the defendant was charged with murder. At the trial, defense counsel, who had been assigned to the case, did not offer any defense based on an alleged attack on the defendant by his victim, according to which the defendant would have been guilty of manslaughter only. Counsel later testified that he did not make the defense because he believed that it was incredible and he could not conscientiously present it to the jury. The defendant attacked his conviction of first-degree murder on the ground that he had not had effective assistance of counsel. The court agreed. It said that had defense counsel avoided the manslaughter theory for tactical reasons, because he thought it would best serve his client, the defendant could not have complained even if it turned out that his lawyer's judgment was mistaken. But defense counsel could not so act on ethical grounds or, it may be presumed, on the ground of any societal interest distinct from the defendant's advantage.[3] The latter conclusion of the court has sometimes been disputed. But it is beyond question that had defense counsel chosen to present the manslaughter theory notwithstanding his disbelief, his conduct would not have been disapproved. Most defense counsel, had they tried the case conscientiously, would have presented the defense; professional conscience so dictates.

Very little of a search for truth survives this definition of the lawyers' roles. It is never an occasion for regret or criticism of defense counsel that he obtained an acquittal or, what is usually sufficient, avoided a conviction. His reputation is based on his ability to "get his client off."* The prosecutor is not expected to be quite as single-mindedly intent on a conviction as defense counsel is on avoiding one. For him also, however, the outcome of the trial is what counts. He views a case in which the jury does not convict or convicts of too minor a crime as a "loss" and wonders how he might have done better. He is never congratulated for an acquittal. He is told at most, rather regretfully, that he did a fine job *but* the verdict "against him" was fair.

THE ADVERSARY SYSTEM

The criminal trial in this country has experienced a gradual, cumulative transformation of the roles of prosecutor and defense counsel from rather narrowly defined aides in a judicial process in which the main responsibilities were those of the judge and jury into the dominant actors in an adversary process which the judge referees and the jury observes. Formerly, the judge frequently played an active

---

*Imagine the response if a defense lawyer should say to his client, "It is true that you were convicted and that you may now spend some time in prison. But wasn't it a splendid trial!"

role in a trial; he might question witnesses, comment on the evidence, and summarize the evidence for the jury. He had an independent responsibility to see that justice was done limited mainly by prerogatives of the jury, which he was expected not to bully. Little of that remains except the theory and some rhetoric. The judge's main function now, aside from keeping order, is to preserve the adversary framework within which the lawyers operate. While he retains authority to intervene in the trial by asking questions and summoning witnesses, he rarely does so; intervention is regarded as interference in the lawyers' work.

The jury's role has likewise diminished. Once regarded as responsible citizens of the community whom the lawyers served, jurors are now credited with small intelligence of their own and must submit to the lawyers' efforts to manipulate them. While there is generally no prohibition against a juror asking questions, none is necessary because the entire structure of the trial inhibits him from doing so; even physically he is separated from the conduct of the trial, placed roughly like a spectator at a theater. The judge's charge to the jury, which might once have been an immediate, direct, and personal communication from him to them and might have included his observations about the trial, is now typically limited to instructions about the law, which he reads from a book of instructions. The lawyers advise him about which instructions to give. Most judges do not depart from the standard instructions, which are ready to hand; to stay close to them avoids the risk of being reversed on appeal. One might formerly have conceived the judge's charge to the jury as the first stage of a collaborative effort to decide the case, the judge then being obliged to withdraw and let the jury reach its verdict without him. There is now no sense of that collaboration.

Such complete and exclusive reliance on partisan presentation of evidence within an adversarial structure does not commend itself to common sense. We do, it is true, in many circumstances rely on advocacy committed to different sides of an issue to help us see points that more neutral consideration might overlook or dismiss. But we do not rely on it so exclusively that there can be no objective presentation or argument at all. The defendant is opposed to the state's purpose when it prosecutes him. It is easy to conclude, therefore, that the principle of adversariness is an inevitable operating principle, not deliberately chosen so much as simply extracted from the circumstances. But participants in a process commonly have adverse individual interests. We far more often try to develop procedures that overcome the opposition between them by substituting a common goal or by making the opposition irrelevant than we make it the hub and rim of the whole wheel. In fact, of course, the defendant is expected to and does cooperate in a great many aspects of a trial. He stands and sits as he is directed. He allows witnesses to study him for identification. He observes the decorum of the courtroom. While that does not tell us when we should rely on cooperation and when we should encourage the defendant to assert his own interest, it does render meaningless the abstract assertion that everything about criminal process is adversary "anyway" because the defendant does not want to be convicted.

Our choice is not abstractly between adversariness and something else. Nor is it concretely, as it is often represented, a choice between our present trial procedures and a process in which the state continues to function as an adversary but the defendant does not, a combat in which one of the combatants is given all the weapons. Overblown rhetoric in praise of "our adversary system" clouds particular issues about how a trial should be conducted, most of which can be answered much more variously than just yes or no. Particularly when some change is proposed, it is commonly asserted that our current procedures are *the* adversary system, so that any departure from what we do now will create another "system" in which the defendant's ability to defend himself against the state will be gone. Less nominalistically, it is sometimes assumed that the kind and amount of adversariness that do serve the objective of a fair search for truth cannot be had except by committing ourselves to adversariness as fully as we do now; such an assumption lurks, for example, in the widely shared but wildly implausible belief that if defense counsel were given access to the prosecution's evidence, he himself would not investigate as hard(!) as he does now. Unspecific and unsupported by either reason or experience, that assumption is as sensible as a question like the following from someone familiar with more violent ways but unfamiliar with football: "But how can you speak of the teams opposing one another if the players are not allowed to kick, punch, or bite?" It is true that if the players are told that they are allowed to do such things and should decide what to do strictly on the basis of what will produce a victory, a well-placed punch will be in order. Similarly, lawyers who are given responsibility for decisions and told that the proper basis for decision is what advances their respective sides cannot be expected to stop short of the limits of professional behavior. But there is no reason to believe that the lines that are currently drawn between "utmost zeal" and unprofessional conduct are the only ones that lawyers can follow or are even the easiest to follow. Certainly the current lines are not easily applied. In other countries, the limits of professional behavior are drawn differently and closer to common sense.

There was a vivid example of the lack of agreement about the boundaries of professional behavior in this country in 1966, when Monroe H. Freedman, a member of the

District of Columbia bar, discussed the following questions at a Criminal Trial Institute:

> 1. Is it proper to cross-examine for the purpose of discrediting the reliability or credibility of an adverse witness whom you know to be telling the truth?
> 2. Is it proper to put a witness on the stand when you know he will commit perjury?
> 3. Is it proper to give your client legal advice when you have reason to believe that the knowledge you give him will tempt him to commit perjury?

He concluded, with some uncertainty, that the nature of the adversary system often required affirmative answers to all three questions. While his conclusion reflects the actual conduct of regular defense counsel in many circumstances—many lawyers manage to conduct themselves in practice so that they do not "know" facts which would make them face such questions head on—he was atypical in refusing to avoid the answers by what he called the "common question-begging responses." Having heard of Mr. Freedman's answers, some federal judges in the District of Columbia urged that he be disbarred. After lengthy proceedings, the matter was dropped.[4] Mr. Freedman later became chairman of the Legal Ethics Committee of the District of Columbia bar.

The adversary system of criminal trial has no independent value for us. It is valuable only insofar as it serves the objectives for which society conducts criminal trials. It does not—or at least we do not care if it does—make the participants or observers healthy, strong, wise, or noble. It is not an occasion for self-expression by the prosecutor or defense counsel or for that matter anyone else, including the defendant, who is involved. To whatever extent our reliance on adversariness is inconsistent with the primary objective of reaching verdicts that reflect accurately the defendant's guilt or innocence, with the proper special emphasis on avoiding an erroneous conviction, it is mistaken. If one insists on giving some weight to the incidental social utilities of a criminal trial that have been suggested—civic education, moral uplift, and so forth—it is nonetheless plain that those benefits are not only subsidiary to but dependent on our maximum achievement of the primary objective. There is not much in civics or morality to be said for convicting the innocent or, some of the guilty being convicted, not convicting others equally guilty and deserving of punishment whom we might convict without convicting the innocent.

Once the matter is placed in that perspective, much of what we now accept as inevitable aspects of an adversary system loses its plausibility. There is no reason why committed, partisan advocacy of a position, including forceful presentation of inferences and arguments for one side, need be attached to partisan presentation of the evidence. There is no reason why witnesses need always be assigned to the prosecution or defense and presented as part of the case for one side, rather than as witnesses to an event. There is no reason why the information that a witness gives need be controlled by someone who is determined to avoid the disclosure of evidence favorable to the other side, however relevant to the inquiry. There is no reason why an intense, searching examination of a witness's recollections to ensure their accuracy need regularly be accompanied by deliberately manipulative efforts to obscure or discredit his testimony; or why the duty to be a witness at a criminal trial should require submission to almost any abusive questioning tactic that an opposing lawyer may devise. There is no reason why rules of procedure designed to ensure a fair trial need systematically be distorted by lawyers into tactical ploys for which they were not intended. A criminal trial need not be from beginning to end an exercise in the tactics of persuasion rather than an effort to come as close as we can to finding out what happened.

There is no "invisible hand" at work to ensure that the social objective of an accurate verdict will be served by the pursuit of independent professional objectives of persons cast insistently and exclusively as adversaries. Unlimited reliance on the independent tactical decisions of defense counsel is particularly inappropriate, since the quality of the decisions often varies according to the defendant's ability to pay. It is plain of course that private lawyers command differential fees and that the highest fees go to those who promise the most; in this situation, "the most" means the best chance for avoiding punishment whether or not one is guilty. Unless we are prepared to assert that a defense lawyer's ability and commitment to his client's cause do not significantly affect his performance at trial or that his performance does not significantly affect the trial's outcome, we should do our utmost to control those aspects of a trial in which his (and the prosecutor's) performance count most. If we are prepared to make those assertions, then the adversary system is topheavy to the extent of them and should be cut down.

While it hardly seems an issue that there are excesses of adversariness that distort a criminal trial, it is not so clear how much the outcome is affected. Most trials are straightforward. The decisions that counsel make do not often affect the verdict, not because there was no room to make a wrong decision, but because it is not so difficult to make decisions that are right enough. Even tasks like cross-examination which lawyers like to describe as an art are usually carried out at the level of a skill; it is not difficult to learn to do them well enough. One may doubt whether the technique and tactics and strategies make much difference in the end, even if they affect the course of the trial. Lawyers themselves assure us that their special competence does make a difference, but except insofar as they obtain random clues from jurors' comments they have no way of telling how much. It is not surprising that the members of a profession, especially those who have been most successful within it, value highly the skills that constitute professional expertise. I doubt that tactics ordinarily matter as much as their use would indicate; the trial is too manifold for the individual or cumulative direction of small tactical pushes to be predictable. The evidence of guilt is often too prosaic and straightforward for there to be much of an issue. Without much more information about how juries deliberate than we have, one can say only that (happily) trial strategy almost certainly is less generally critical to the result than lawyers assert.

Equally certain, however, trial strategy sometimes is critical. And whether or not the outcome is changed by tactical maneuvers, the trial is debased. Attention is shifted from its proper focus on the defendant's conduct. Our concentration on the lawyers, neither of whom is involved except professionally, makes it inevitable that everyone, not least the defendant, will perceive the issue as win or lose rather than provably guilty or not. Even if the defendant committed the crime charged, we cannot expect him to acknowledge the justice of a conviction if he believes that the outcome of the trial depends as much on the tactics and strategies of the lawyers as it does on his actual guilt and that the trial is knowingly so designed.

The critical relationships that ought to determine the structure of a trial are between the defendant and the witnesses, on whose evidence the verdict depends; between the defendant and the jury, and the witnesses and the jury, which has responsibility for the verdict; and between the defendant and the judge, who must impose sentence if the defendant is convicted. None of those relationships now exists at all, except as it is deliberately shaped by the lawyers and filtered through the irrelevant adversary relationship between them. The defendant has almost no role. Protective of his right to be present and insistent on his duty to be present, we nevertheless require him to be entirely passive. He has the right to testify as a witness subject to the same conditions as other witnesses; like them, his testimony is given under oath, is elicited in response to his lawyer's questions, and is subject to cross-examination. He has no right and is never allowed to speak not as a witness, but as a person who has been accused of a crime. He may not personally challenge a witness, or contradict him, or ask for detail. The defendant's constitutional right "to be confronted with the witnesses against him" is interpreted narrowly and technically as a right to know the state's evidence and cross-examine its witnesses.

Simply as an aid to factfinding, there should be an opportunity for the defendant himself to *confront* the state's witnesses. A direct confrontation between an accused and the witnesses for the prosecution (or between witnesses who have given conflicting testimony) is a powerful means to elicit a convincing account of what actually happened. If they are accustomed to the rigidly structured testimony of witnesses at an American trial, observers of a trial where that occurs may be startled by the value of such an exchange in the courtroom. Beyond that, respect for the defendant as a responsible individual, still a member of the society that prosecutes him, demands that he not be treated merely as an object at his trial. The power to challenge the accusation, to assert oneself and be recognized within the trial, is not fulfilled by a stranger's questions however acute the questions and partisan the stranger.

Defense counsel is neither the defendant's alter ego nor his "champion," as the legal profession likes to describe him. He is a professional functionary necessary to the process by which the defendant is prosecuted, who works within the system not in opposition to it. Defendants understand this, and often show little appreciation or affection for their lawyer even after a favorable verdict. Defense lawyers learn not to expect gratitude, which too often would be out of place in the circumstances. We speak usually as if it is the defendant who defends, counseled by his lawyer. More accurately, one would say that it is defense counsel who defends with the help of the defendant. But that too is a distortion. Defense counsel rarely has the time or inclination to consult with his client on strategic matters or to respond to his suggestions. Since all that counts is whether the case is won or lost, the defendant has no reason to oppose his lawyer's professional judgment. Facing the inconsistency between our rhetoric and the reality, courts have recognized more and more that the defendant may have as little control over, and as little right to control, "his" counsel as he does the prosecutor. We have come full circle. The defendant's hard-won rights to keep silent and to be advised and represented by counsel have become effectively a barrier to his participation in his own trial, justified on the ground that he has a lawyer to defend him.

The defendant's subservience to the two-sided model of a trial is matched by the jury's. Selected by a more rigorous examination than anywhere else in the world and insulated after their verdict from almost any inquiry into their deliberations, jurors sit during the trial as passive auditors and spectators to whatever the prosecutor and defense counsel put before them. The jurors must decide what happened; but they ask no questions, pursue no lines of inquiry of their own, indicate none of their doubts, obtain no clarification. The use in this country of a jury composed exclusively of lay persons has contributed to the jurors' exclusion from participation in the trial. Elsewhere, the verdict is rendered by a panel of professional and lay persons (called "lay judges") who may all participate in the trial, although a professional judge presides and takes primary responsibility for questioning witnesses. Relying as fully as we do on the good sense of jurors in other respects, there is no reason why they should not be encouraged to ask questions of witnesses within the bounds of orderly procedure. That persons who decide a factual controversy ought be able to ask questions material to their decision seems indeed so obvious that it should scarcely be an issue. The real source of objection to such a practice is that the jurors' occasional interventions would leave the conduct of a trial less exclusively in the control of the lawyers and change it somewhat from a contest between the lawyers into a factual inquiry that the jurors resolve.

The physical configuration of a trial is a close approximation of its content. All the action takes place in a central space like an arena, which is separated from the public part of the courtroom by the "bar," from the judge by the "bench" which rises above the arena and encloses him (and often also by desks for court officials that surround the bench like foothills), and from the jurors, who are enclosed in a "box" of their own off to one side. The prosecutor and defense counsel sit at tables in the arena. The defendant sits, seen but not heard, at the table with his lawyer. When they testify, witnesses sit facing the lawyer who questions them. All the participants except the two lawyers remain seated throughout the trial; they rise only to pass to and from their assigned places. The lawyers stand when they speak. They roam around and draw all attention to themselves. It is their arena and they determine what happens in it.

SENTENCE

Sometime after the trial, usually within about two weeks, the trial judge imposes sentence on a defendant who has been found guilty. Commonly, the judge is aided by a presentence report prepared by a probation officer or some other person attached to the court. The report contains information about the defendant's criminal record, family background, education, work history, reputation, "attitudes," and other details that the officer puts together from public records and interviews with the defendant and others. The judge receives the report and studies it before the sentencing hearing. While the prosecutor and defense counsel may be allowed to examine the report and challenge its findings and recommendations, there is no adversary presentation of the information itself. Usually, the judge's decision about the sentence is effectively made before the hearing.

Neither the nature of the issue nor the kind of evidence that is used makes an administrative, nonadversary proceeding more appropriate for determining the sentence than for determining guilt. The judge's discretion generally is very large. Many, probably most, defendants whose cases reach judgment are more concerned about the sentence than whether or not they will be found guilty. The information on which the sentence is based often is more evanescent and uncertain than the testimony at trial. The manner of determining sentence is itself far from a model of intelligent, fair procedure. Our willingness to dispense with all the paraphernalia of the adversary system as soon as the trial is over suggests, however, how little its domination of the trial is a product of considered choice.

In all but the rarest cases, the use of presentence reports has meant simply delay. They are a product of the penal theory that sentences should be "individualized" to let the punishment fit the criminal rather than the crime. The theory has a humanitarian purpose. But we lack both the understanding and the means to adjust sentences very much to any but the most readily available data, mostly the defendant's age, the nature of the crime, and his prior record of criminal behavior. Without more adequate understanding about what the relevant "individualizing" circumstances should be, the demand of even-handed justice should prevail; persons who commit the same crime in similar circumstances should be punished alike. Much more would be accomplished, with considerably more justice and no less humanity, if the range of sentences were sharply narrowed, the maximum sentence greatly reduced, and the imposition of a definite sentence made to follow swiftly and certainly from proof of guilt. If the statutory sentencing provisions themselves were made more definite (and sentences reduced), in most cases it would be practicable to impose sentence at the same time that the verdict was rendered, which should be the normal practice. The few central facts on which narrowed sentencing discretion would rest could be ascertained routinely before trial.

6

AN ALTERNATIVE MODEL

The deficiencies of the criminal process have a common strand. Notwithstanding our preoccupation with law and order and the rights of the individual, our thinking about criminal justice is dominated by an abstract model which has little relation to what actually happens. In practice, the criminal process has been an incidental concern of institutions, the police and the legal profession, which have other primary interests. There has been more than enough rhetoric about criminal justice on all sides, from politicians and scholars as well as lawyers. There has been no end of tinkering with detail, by the courts above all. Grand rhetoric and small tinkering alike have not challenged or even paid much attention to the underlying framework of investigation by the police and prosecution according to the adversary model of private litigation. Since that framework is unsound, it is not surprising that most observers conclude finally that

117

the criminal process cannot be improved very much and that the most one can achieve is a temporary leaning to one side or another, a bit more law enforcement or a bit more respect for the defendant. Only slightly removed from that frustrating dead end is the conclusion that a significant improvement in the quality of criminal justice would require us to commit resources which the country does not have or at any rate does not want to spend in that way; we must work within the bounds of the present system because realistically we cannot afford a better one.

Criminal justice will never be anything but an unpleasant social necessity; there is no way to accomplish it joyfully. Nor can one ignore the difficulty of large institutional change, especially if the institutions in question are as established and powerful as the police and the legal profession. But it is not true that we cannot devise a more rational criminal process. It is not true that any better process would cost too much. It is not true that whatever process we devised would only reflect another particular set of preferences without bringing us closer to our common objectives.

The major features of a reconstructed criminal process are described in this chapter. The institutional arrangements for carrying it out are unfamiliar in the United States; but they are used in one form or another throughout the world. While the choice of these arrangements out of all the possible ways of going about the investigation and prosecution of crime is no doubt encouraged by their actual use elsewhere, the particular form that I have given them here is dictated by the arguments presented earlier about the inadequacy of our present practices. Unlikely as some of the recommendations may appear, they are the implications of objectives about which we all agree. The two central recommendations are (1) that the investigative responsibility of the police, except insofar as it is an incidental aspect of their peacekeeping and emergency functions, be reassigned to an independent branch of the judiciary, and (2) that primary responsibility for investigating a crime, preparing an accusation, and proving guilt be joined in a single agency. Both recommendations call for the creation of an investigating magistracy, a public institution unknown in this country. The outline which follows is intended to be more than an elegant hypostatization of abstract principles. It is the general institutional structure that is important, however, and not its precise implementation, which only our own experience can supply.

INVESTIGATION

What was once the luxury of a public police force that could respond to public and private emergencies is now a necessity for any large urban community in this country. Consideration of the role of the police in the criminal process has to start from the premise that their peacekeeping and general emergency services will continue to be their first and largest responsibility and, therefore, will determine the characteristics of the police as a public institution. We shall not, and should not, dispense with police organized, trained, and equipped to act swiftly and forcefully at the scene of a disturbance, criminal or not. On the contrary, our effort has been and will continue to be to increase just that capacity of the police, which directly affects the security of our lives.

That is our starting point. It follows reasonably that the police are not able to carry out as we should like the demands of criminal process which we now assign to them. We cannot expect the same public officials to act in dangerous, violent, unpredictable, and uncertain circumstances with the minimum of harm to themselves or others and also to act judiciously, with discretion, and mindful of conflicting interests. Still less can we expect them to fulfill both expectations if persons who put the police in danger and whom they must often subdue by force in one capacity are the same persons whom they are asked to treat with dignity and respect in the other. Our courts have too often been willing to urge that the police acquire the habits of judges; it is not surprising that the police react by suggesting that the judges might like to take on some of the duties of the police.

When the police are asked to respond to a disturbed situation, often there is a choice to be made between an effective peacekeeping response and the value of an unintrusive government in a free society. Usually, the choice is not simply one or the other, but how much of one at what sacrifice of the other. Whatever choice is made will leave some dissatisfaction. In order not to authorize too much intrusion, we may choose not to treat a situation as a true emergency. So, for example, we restrict the authority of the police to accost suspicious persons on the street, even though if they were allowed to do so more often some additional crimes would be prevented. If we do choose to treat the situation as an emergency, it follows from that choice both that the police are the appropriate agency to respond and that the response will not be carried out with the circumspection of reasoned discussion and orderly procedures. The fact that the situation is an emergency, which is the reason for calling in the police instead of some other agency, also explains why the response will be less cautious than other circumstances would allow.

Many of the situations to which the police respond as keepers of the peace involve crimes. Often their response has consequences for criminal process. When they arrest someone who is fleeing from the scene of a mugging, they not only restore order; they identify a criminal. When they ask the victim or witnesses "what happened" after the mugger has fled, that helps to restore order and calms people, but at the same time, they are gathering information that may be useful later in a prosecution. So far as such results flow from police actions that are legitimated by their other responsibilities, primarily peacekeeping, criminal process is an incidental beneficiary, and considerations about criminal process do not much affect the way the police behave. We may allow it to benefit from their actions or not; but the way they act will not be much changed if we do not.

There is another kind of situation in which there is no emergency except for some need of the criminal process, which is expected to benefit directly from the police action. When, for example, the police make an arrest primarily in order to search, they may have to make a swift, forceful encounter on the street. But the need is functionally related to the criminal process: it arises only because the police want to seize evidence of a crime before the person has disposed of it. One of the persistent objections to police behavior is that this kind of "emergency," when the police are primarily interested in obtaining evidence, is explained differently. A "protective frisk" which an officer claims was necessary to avert an imminent danger to himself or others too often appears to have been a search for illegal drugs rather than weapons. Since the police have responsibility for both peacekeeping and criminal investigation, it is not easy for them or us to keep the two kinds of "emergency" clearly separate. However, if we conclude that the need of the criminal process is great enough to justify "emergency" investigative techniques like a sudden search, then again it is plain that the police are the appropriate agency and that they will act as the emergency requires.

It is just as plain that we ought not to rely on the police when circumstances do not require it. Their special characteristics are at once costly and unsuited to public responsibilities that do not depend on swift, mobile, and forceful action. We may be glad that a police officer can give first aid in an emergency; but no one supposes that it is preferable to perform an operation on the sidewalk if there is time and opportunity to get the person to a hospital. Similarly, the fact that we count on the police to stop a crime and make an arrest in a disordered situation is not a reason for counting on them further after order is restored and the man is in custody. Nor is it a reason why, once a crime is over and there is no longer a peacekeeping function to perform, we should leave it to the police to decide when to arrest and what investigations to undertake, any more than we rely on them to perform a medical operation that can be planned in advance.

There is now no alternative to the police as an official investigative agency. To return once more to the medical comparison, it is as if we had police equipped to give first aid but no public hospitals; in the circumstances, we should expect cruder medicine and fewer recoveries than we have now. Rather than leave the responsibilities to the police and try to teach them to be judges, the sensible solution is to create a public office with the attributes we want it to have and give it responsibility for criminal investigation in non-emergency conditions.

When the police have left the scene of a crime with the (apparent) criminal in custody, their independent authority and responsibility to conduct an investigation involving him should end. The need for an immediate response at the scene of the crime is over. None of the steps taken at the police station—booking, questioning, lineups, and so forth—needs to be carried out there. If police are able to take a person to the police station and detain him there for several hours, they can as easily take him someplace else. In order to terminate their custody, they should take the person *directly* from the place of the arrest before a judicial official, a magistrate. That is what the law formally prescribes now. But the police go to the magistrate by way of the stationhouse, where they complete their investigation and prepare the police report. If the responsibility for all of the tasks now performed at the police station were expressly assigned elsewhere, the reason for going there at all with an arrested person would be gone. The need to quiet an emergency on the street does not dictate where a man shall be taken for the performance of tasks of that kind.

From every point of view, it would be an improvement if routine clerical tasks like booking and fingerprinting and investigative tasks like lineups and questioning were entrusted to a judicial officer instead of the police. The courts have repeatedly stated our preference to get an arrested person out of the custody of the police as soon as we can. Accustomed and expected to use force, the police represent more than any other civil institution the physical power of the state. Especially in the context of an arrest, which involves at least an involuntary restraint and frequently the actual use of force, prolongation of the encounter with the police prolongs the state's application of force to the individual, needlessly if the use of force is no longer appropriate. Not only does continued police custody increase the likelihood that some degree of actual force will be used unnecessarily; even if the behavior of the police is restrained, the arrested person is likely to see their custody of him itself as an application of force. A magistrate also represents the state, but in a different guise. The physical trappings of the judiciary are different from those of a police station; they manifest authority and law, not force. Unlike the police, the magistrate would not have participated in the arrest.

It has always been somewhat fatuous for the courts to insist that the police at the police station should act as legal counselor to someone whom they have just arrested and give him substantial advice about how to assert his rights against themselves. Given all our other expectations of them, we cannot expect neutrality of that kind. We could, however, expect a magistrate who does not have the peacekeeping and emergency responsibilities of the police to follow a more neutral course. His first obligation on presentation of an arrested person would be, as it is now, to assure him that he is no longer in the custody of the police and that he will be afforded the due process of the law with the specific rights that the law guarantees.

At the time that a person is taken before him, the magistrate should require the arresting officer to make an oral statement in the presence of the person of the reason for and circumstances of the arrest. The statement should describe briefly the evidence of the crime (as in the arrest report) and refer explicitly to physical evidence taken from the person and incriminating statements that he made. The magistrate should ask questions to resolve obvious ambiguities and doubts. At the same time, he should offer the person himself an opportunity to ask the police officer questions and to contradict him. The magistrate should ask the person explicitly whether he was abused by the police.

At the police station, where he is detained only to accomplish the state's investigative purpose, a person who is arrested cannot be other than an object, a source of information. Before the magistrate, interposed between him and the police, he can be a participant in a fair procedure designed partly for his protection. Someone who is caught in the act or just after may have small need for an account of his crime. But it will help to make his situation clear if he hears the state's case at the earliest moment. Giving him a prompt opportunity to listen and to speak before the magistrate will both emphasize the state's purpose to prosecute him if he is guilty and assure him that he is not unprotected. For obvious reasons, no inquiry about police abuse is made at the police station. But unless we provide for an effective inquiry promptly after an encounter with the police (rather than months later in the course of prosecution, as we do now), our expressions of concern about their conduct will remain largely theoretical and unconvincing. The police are less likely to violate their office if they may be called to account literally within the hour. Descriptions of what happened are likely to be much more credible and in fact accurate if they are given before the passage of time fades and recolors them.

The magistrate should have the authority now exercised by the police to carry out whatever aspects of booking are worth preserving and to conduct lineups and other identification procedures. Unlike the police, whose authority depends on a prior arrest and ends with it, a magistrate would not be obliged to act hastily if the procedure could be carried out in a more reliable or dignified or convenient way later; his judicial authority would allow him to release a person subject to a duty to reappear. Submission to any such procedure would be based on the duty to respond to a judicial order rather than the bare exercise of forceful authority by the police.

Limited to their peacekeeping function, the authority of the police should not extend independently to arrest or investigation. If they make no arrest at the scene of a crime, once their peacekeeping function is performed their responsibility should require and their authority permit only that they report the crime and whatever evidence they have to the appropriate magistrate. It should be part of his office to decide whether and, if so, how to investigate further. Further investigative steps by the police would be subject to his authority and supervision. That approach contrasts sharply with our present practices, which, except for search warrants, make no regular provision for judicial supervision of investigation. Unwanted intrusions in our lives should not be within the uncontrolled discretion of the police if the purpose is investigation of crime any more than if it is some other purpose, unless circumstances do not allow an opportunity for more careful judgment and more circumspect official behavior.

The principle that criminal investigation should be conducted within bounds set by balanced, magisterial judgment is well established. It is confirmed whenever the courts indicate the standard by which they test behavior of the police. The *office* of an investigating magistracy is unfamiliar in this country, and contradicts our accustomed separation of prosecutorial and judicial functions. It is easy to suppose that the establishment of an investigating magistracy would pointlessly multiply entities and that the magistrate would simply be—and act like—the police, with a different title and different clothing. Because our concern for the manner of investigation has been expressed so much in terms of its results, the critical issue usually being the admissibility of evidence, it is easy to dismiss the differences between a magistrate and the police if the former would have the same investigative authority as the latter now have. While we could, of course, make such a change in name only, which would be pointless or worse, it is surely a gratuitous assumption, unsupported by our experience, that it must be so. Differences in organization and training, professional identification, and physical surroundings and, above all, separation of the magistrate's proceedings from the entirely different tasks of keeping the peace and preserving public order would all have effect. It is, after all, differences of that kind that make "all the difference" between, say, police interrogation and judicial examination of a witness. None of us would hesitate to reject the suggestion that a police officer should be allowed to substitute for a judge at trial; the same reasons urge substitution of a magistrate for the police officer once the emergency and forceful encounter on the street are over.

The strongest objection to magisterial investigation may come from the side of the accused, based on fear that a magistrate's responsibility to "clear" cases will affect him as it does the police and make him not neutral. Experience in other countries suggests that while prosecutorial bias is not an inevitable feature of an investigating magistracy, it ought to be taken seriously into account. It needs to be emphasized, therefore, that the magistrate's investigating responsibilities would replace the responsibility of the police as investigators and not responsibilities or prerogatives of the defense or the trial judge or jury. If a magistracy could not be counted on invariably to meet as exacting a standard of neutrality as we should like, we could surely count on it to come considerably closer than the police do.

Having given the police the primary task of guarding our peace and security, we can no more expect them to perform magisterial functions than we can—or do—expect a judge who tries criminal cases also to respond in a squad car when the bank alarm goes off. Unless we have in mind some function which demands the special characteristics of the police, we should not subject persons, even persons who probably have committed a crime, to their nonneutral, nonprotective custody. The issue is fairly debatable only in those terms. Absent emergency, if we do not have the use of force in mind, the police are not an appropriate agency to carry out our purpose. They would not readily relinquish their role as crime fighters. But they would be restored to their original, primary role as protectors of the peace of the community and a resource in emergencies. Their identification as crime fighters has had effects on them and the public generally which impede relationships of confidence and reliance. Good police-community relationships will not spring into being from creation of an investigating magistracy. They will, however, be encouraged by the clear identification of the police department as a service agency, which in fact it always has been.

Magisterial responsibility would not necessarily affect the amount of investigative work that is done. Most often, there would continue to be little more than the routine, uncomplicated, and expeditious collection of information at the scene of a crime, which the police would do, as now, as part of their peacekeeping duties. The difficulties that frustrate investigation of banal, anonymous crimes would not be eliminated. We could not expect a magistrate, any more than we now expect the police, to investigate most crimes of that kind that are not cleared directly by the criminal's apprehension in the act. The police report to the magistrate of an unsolved crime ordinarily would effectively close the case. It would be his responsibility, as it is now the responsibility of the police, to decide which cases to investigate further.

When an investigation is pursued, just as the victim of a crime and witnesses are interviewed now at the police station, they would be interviewed by the magistrate in his office. If the (apparent) criminal were apprehended at the scene, witnesses would often be able to accompany the police officer when he brought the person before the magistrate. We are accustomed to prompt action of that kind by the police but not by the judiciary, which proceeds at a more leisurely pace. Plainly, there is no reason why witnesses should not appear before a magistrate as promptly as they do now at the police station. At the same time, in place of the impromptu practices on which the police rely, when it was necessary a magistrate's power to investigate would rest directly on his judicial authority to summon persons for examination. In that respect his authority would be similar to that of a grand jury presently. By a specific authorization, he might delegate a task that had to be carried out away from his office and required only the execution of a defined responsibility, as search warrants now authorize the police to make a search.* He should be required to perform personally tasks like questioning witnesses that depend on judicial attributes. A magistracy would need the support of trained personnel: technical experts like medical examiners, laboratory analysts, and photographers; field investigators; and clerical assistance. The tasks of criminal investigation call for such people whether it is performed by the police or a magistracy.

A central feature of magisterial investigation in other countries is usually the magistrate's examination of the accused. In this country, the constitutional privilege against compulsory self-incrimination has provided a doctrinal barrier to extended questioning of suspects. The more concrete basis for not allowing such questioning as a standard practice is that there has been no one except the police to do it. The courts have rightly concluded that police questioning should be strictly limited if not indeed prohibited altogether. While the different circumstances of magisterial investigation do not require that the oral examination of suspects be allowed, they do considerably affect the issue.

Any questioning of an accused person should be conducted with the incidents of a judicial proceeding, not a

---

*Within the existing process, the combination of prosecutorial and judicial authority in the hands of a prosecuting official such as a district attorney violates our right not to be subject to certain kinds of investigative procedure, including a search, without neutral judicial authorization. The grand jury, on the other hand, combines aspects of prosecutorial and judicial authority. Were we to establish an investigating magistracy, our present categories of "investigative," "prosecutorial," and "judicial" authority plainly would not be transferable unchanged.

"stationhouse interrogation." The magistrate should advise the suspect that he is not obliged to say anything about the crime whether he is guilty or not, and that there will be no effort to make him say anything by manipulation or trickery. The advice should be given substantially and not as a formal preliminary to increasingly intensive questioning, as it too often is at the police station. But it would also be normal and proper for the magistrate to state that it is his task to investigate the crime and that he is asking questions as part of his recognized official duties. Questioning should normally be conducted in the presence of a suspect's lawyer, to reassure the suspect and us that the magistrate's questions did not exceed proper inquiry. The lawyer should be permitted with great liberality to suggest lines of questioning to the magistrate, to point out ambiguities in questions, and to help the magistrate resolve confusions. It would not be any part of his function at the hearing to advise his client to be silent; nor would it be proper for him to give that advice to his client privately. On the other hand, if the magistrate browbeat his client or were overbearing, it would be the lawyer's duty to object then and later. It should not be a bar to questioning a person that his lawyer is not present; but if he declined for that reason to respond, that should be an end of the matter, simply because he does not have to respond whatever his reasons.*

Unfamiliarity with the conception of an investigating magistracy may engender objections and doubts which responses to hypothetical questions will not be able to satisfy. There are models in other countries from which we can gain confidence and borrow many details; but none of them is

---

*I have set forth in the Appendix, page 147, an argument that questioning conducted by a magistrate along these lines would be consistent with the values protected by the privilege against self-incrimination.

fully suited to our circumstances, and they give rise to objections of their own. Without experience of our own to go on, the most general response to objections is also the strongest. When the courts have tried to develop standards for investigation which allow officials enough authority to carry out essential functions without disregarding individual rights, their effort has been frustrated by the nature of the police as an institution. If the premises that determine our choice of investigative process are taken seriously, their implementation calls for establishment of another institution. Whether or not we use the unfamiliar concept of "magisterial investigation," that is in fact what our premises describe. If the police behaved as we say they should, that would be magisterial investigation. They cannot be expected to behave that way because we have another set of inconsistent expectations which are primary. If the comparison is made with actual police practices, which it would replace, the case for magisterial investigation is very strong indeed. If no such comparison is made, objections to a magistracy are, after all, rather empty.

The present division of responsibility between the police and the prosecutor has the dual effect of excluding the defendant and his counsel from the principal investigation of a crime and, on the government's side, separating the investigation from the formal accusation which follows. The circumstances of ordinary police work do not lend themselves to the participation of lawyers. Accustomed to act quickly, the police do not readily allow their actions to be attended and observed by others, especially those like defense counsel who can reasonably be expected to obstruct them if they can. So long as the police develop the evidence of a crime, therefore, the investigation will be directed against the defendant, not only in the sense that he is an object of suspicion but also in the sense that he is shut out from the investigation.

The state's investigation of a crime is substantially complete before the defendant has a significant opportunity or occasion to develop evidence in his own behalf. He receives from the state at most the product of its prior investigative work, which carries no assurance that it includes all that might be favorable to him. Accordingly, after the investigation by the state is completed, the defendant is given an opportunity to conduct his own investigation. Almost always there is little investigation for him to do, just as in fact the police seldom conduct an extensive investigation either. But his opportunity cannot be denied, especially since the investigation by the police is not seriously concerned to uncover information that might ambiguously cast doubt on their conclusions.

The prosecutor receives automatically the information that defense counsel has to request or demand in court. But doing little investigative work on his own and relying on the police report, so far as concerns his individual capacity to form a judgment about the defendant's guilt, the prosecutor is in no position to make a serious, specific accusation. All he can do is protect his absence of judgment by including the maximum charges that the most general view of the evidence might sustain. Instead of determining the defendant's guilt reliably at the earliest possible moment, our present criminal process thus postpones that determination until the last possible moment—and then usually makes it on the basis of a negotiated plea that avoids the need for specific findings altogether.

Transfer of investigative responsibility from the police to a legally trained judicial officer allows unification of the independent investigations of the prosecution and defense into a single investigation, the outcome of which is a careful conclusion supported by the evidence. Once a suspect has been identified, whether or not he has been arrested he should ordinarily be informed of and allowed to participate in further investigative proceedings, including the magistrate's examination of witnesses. Defense counsel and, if the state chooses, a representative of the prosecutor's office should also be allowed to attend. The declared purpose of the investigation should be to find out what happened, not to develop a case for either side. Authority to conduct the examination and primary responsibility for its completeness and accuracy should belong unequivocally to the magistrate. The roles of prosecutor and defense counsel in an investigation, therefore, should not be conceived primarily as those of partisan advocates of a particular result, but as those of aides to the magistrate: to suggest witnesses who should be examined, indicate lines of inquiry, and see that relevant issues are not overlooked. Their additional responsibility would be to ensure by their presence that the magistrate performed his responsibility fairly. As the defendant's representative, defense counsel would be concerned primarily to protect the defendant's rights and to make certain that he have a full opportunity to contest the charges against him. The prosecutor would guard against the too casual or hasty dismissal of the state's interest in criminal prosecution.

Firm magisterial responsibility for a neutral, complete, and convincing investigation departs sharply from our current practices, which do not lodge that responsibility anywhere. One who has those practices in mind may speculate that subordination of prosecutor and defense counsel to the magistrate will prove to be unworkable, and that either their roles will be diminished to uselessness by too strong a magistrate or they will regain their domination of the proceedings. That has not been the invariable experience in other countries, nor need it be here. So long as the principles were firmly established that the magistrate was responsible for the conduct of the proceedings and their result and that the prosecutor and defense counsel had a subordinate but independent responsibility to guard against error or bias, a workable balance could be reached.

Just as at present, most investigations would be straightforward and would be concluded quickly. Investigative procedures are seldom time-consuming in themselves. Witnesses can usually be interviewed without long advance notice; interviews rarely need last as long as an hour. In ordinary cases, including most of those in which the police in the exercise of their peacekeeping function brought someone before the magistrate, all the material evidence would be assembled easily within twenty-four hours. While the investigation of some crimes would be prolonged, a system of magisterial investigation which was freed from the constraints of a totally adversary process and which included a suspect and his lawyer in the investigation from the beginning would be able to complete the investigation of most crimes within a day or two following an arrest.*

ACCUSATION

In place of the bare indictment or information unsupported by any official record of evidence that we have now, a magistrate who has conducted a thorough investigation in which lawyers for the defendant and, if the prosecutor's office wishes, the state have participated will be able to make

---

*Plainly, an investigation could not be expedited that much if the individual schedules of private counsel were accommodated as they are now. We could not adopt a process of magisterial investigation and at the same time reserve to the defendant's lawyer all of his existing prerogatives.

a serious recommendation for disposition of the case. If he has found insufficient basis for an accusation, he should enter an order closing the investigation.* If he has found proof of a crime, he should close the investigation with an order making a specific accusation against the defendant. The accusation should not be merely a formal preliminary to judgment, but the magistrate's legally competent finding that the defendant is guilty of the crime specified.

The evidence that a magistrate has compiled and his order closing the investigation with or without an accusation (accompanied sometimes by a statement of his reasons) will constitute an investigative record of the case. Included in the record should be descriptions (or photographs) of physical evidence, laboratory reports, reports of investigative procedures carried out at the direction of the magistrate, the magistrate's record of investigations made by him personally (such as a view of the scene of the crime), and records of the testimony of all witnesses including the accused if he has been examined. Comparable, albeit less complete, records of a police investigation exist now in one form or another and are collected informally and unofficially in the police file and later the prosecutor's file. They have no evidentiary significance unless they are produced (and, usually, made the subject of oral testimony) at a trial. In most cases, therefore, there is no official, recorded foundation for a verdict of guilt beyond the defendant's plea. In cases that are tried, proof of guilt is hidden in an untranscribed stenographic record or, if there is a transcript, in the procedure and strategies of the trial. It is easy for time to dull the clarity and certainty of guilt. We should have the record of the magistrate's investigation as continuing substantiation of the accusation. At the

---

*Such an order should be subject to an appeal by the office of the prosecutor, if it concluded that the state's interest required further investigation or that there should be an accusation on the basis of the previous investigation.

same time, the requirement that the evidence be a part of the record will help to ensure that an accusation is not unfounded.

Having taken such steps to ensure the reliability of the magistrate's accusation, we should be the more able to rely on it as an element in a final judgment. The converse is also true. By giving the accusation significance for the outcome, we increase the likelihood that the investigation will be complete and reliable. Were the accusation to count for as little as an indictment or information does now, predictably (and reasonably) the magistrate's labor would diminish; whatever the theory about how he ought to conduct an investigation, his actual practices would decline to the level necessary to support the small weight of his results. Accordingly, the accusation should be regarded not as a merely formal preliminary to a distinct and self-contained proceeding to judgment, but as itself an essential component of a criminal conviction. The accusation should be based on the magistrate's own conclusion that beyond a reasonable doubt the defendant is guilty.

The office of the magistrate would thus bring together functions now shared among the police as investigators and the prosecutor, defense counsel, and judiciary as the officials responsible for initiating a prosecution, responding to it, and preparing for trial. From any point of view the objectives of criminal justice would be better served. The standards of fair and reliable investigation would be met far more easily in the atmosphere of a judicial office than in a police station. The unofficial, incomplete, and imprecise police report accompanied by a *pro forma* indictment or information would be replaced by a specific accusation, based on recorded evidence, that informed the defendant of the state's actual purpose against him. Instead of the spasmodic, sequential investigation by the police and much later (if at all) by prosecution and defense and the constricted, reluctant disclosure of evidence before trial, the defendant and his lawyer as well as the state's lawyer would be able to participate in an investigation, recommend investigative measures, and have immediate access to a record of all the evidence. Completion of the magistrate's investigation would depend on the nature of the case and his own schedule, rather than on the independently determined schedules of the opposed lawyers. Ordinarily, therefore, the delay of months that now elapse between an arrest and trial would be unnecessary.

What will have been lost? For the community, nothing. However strangely the proposal for an investigating magistrate may sit among our traditional assumptions, it meets our objectives better than the present haphazardly coordinated institutional arrangements. The main source of skepticism may be fear that a magistrate would have too much power, acquired at the expense of the defendant. Before yielding to that fear, we should test it by specifics and compare a magistracy with what it would replace. In one respect only would defendants be less well off. The vagaries of our current practice would be eliminated and the connection between crime and prosecution made more swift and certain. There would, therefore, be less opportunity to avoid a prosecution or conviction by good luck or accident or legal manipulation. From the point of view of the community, or simply as a matter of criminal justice, that is plainly a desirable result

JUDGMENT

Once the magistrate has made an accusation, the prosecution should move swiftly to judgment. So long as the defense counsel has participated in the magistrate's proceedings, has had an opportunity to recommend investigative steps that ought to be taken, and knows the evidence, it should not be necessary to investigate further after the magistrate has accused the defendant. His order should close the investigation rather than open it. The magistrate's file should also resolve contested legal issues like joinder of offenses and exclusion of evidence.

The fact that there is a specific accusation based on evidence available in the record would eliminate the basis for negotiation of a guilty plea. Even so, it is unlikely that defendants would invariably contest their guilt. If a defendant had participated in the investigation and the accusation were precise and firmly based, and if criminal process acquired the characteristics of swiftness, certainty, and, above all, justice that it now lacks, often he could be expected to admit the facts found by the magistrate—to "get it over with," to avoid embarrassment, or for more complex psychological reasons. In such circumstances the inquiry into the facts of the crime that is described hereafter as part of the proceeding to judgment could be abbreviated, but not eliminated. Whatever the defendant's posture, it is the government's obligation to ensure that a judgment of conviction is accurate.*

Once we depart from the existing model of a criminal trial, it is not so clear who or how many persons should have responsibility for the final determination of guilt or innocence. Our use of twelve lay jurors unaided by any professional judgment has its source in history, not reason. While

*There is, of course, no guarantee that informal arrangements akin to plea bargaining would not develop. An overworked magistrate might accept a suspect's "confession" to a lesser crime as sufficient evidence for an accusation without pursuing further inculpatory (or exculpatory) leads. If the court then accepted the accusation in the perfunctory way that courts now accept a plea of guilty, the magistrate's incomplete performance of his responsibility would be confirmed. We can find ways, if we choose, to reject our own procedures.

it is theoretically possible to design experiments that would indicate what size and composition of juries would be most effective, as a practical matter we are not likely to carry out experiments that would yield persuasive results. In order to take the discussion beyond speculative abstractions, I propose that the functions presently assigned to the judge and jury be fulfilled by a *court* composed of a professional judge, who would preside; two persons who are practicing members of the bar but not professional judges; and seven lay persons who are not members of the legal profession or regularly judges.[1]

The presiding judge would be familiar with the magistrate's file and have primary responsibility for the conduct of the proceeding to judgment. It can be argued that he should preside at the proceeding but not participate in the judgment, as a judge now presides but is not a member of the jury. But he would perform his responsibilities as presiding officer more fully and conscientiously if he had some responsibility also for the outcome. His involvement and professional qualifications would contribute to an accurate judgment. However, the same attributes that would make him a valuable judge disqualify him from judging alone. Having studied the record, he would have an opinion about the verdict in advance of the proceeding. In a matter of such profound importance to the individual defendant, the state should guard with special care against occasional error because of the inadequacy of a particular official. There is also symbolic value in the denial of final power to a single person.

To balance the presiding judge's authority, there should be other persons on the court with professional qualifications and confidence. It should be a professional obligation of persons regularly engaged in the practice of law that they sit as members of a court on a rotating basis, much as we require ordinary persons (not including lawyers) to sit on juries now.* Both to reduce the risk of idiosyncracy from random assignments and to create enough strength in numbers to offset the institutional authority of the judge, two lawyers should sit on the court.

There are also nonprofessional virtues. While training and experience are likely to lead to accurate results in ordinary cases, they may mislead in extraordinary ones. To avoid the limitations of professionalism and to preserve a visible indication of the community's responsibility for criminal justice, the court should include competent, not professionally qualified persons like those who serve as jurors now. To have the benefit of individual idiosyncracies without allowing them too much weight and to make up in numbers the professional strength of the other members of the court, there should be some number of lay jurors more than three—say, seven.

The requirements for a verdict of guilty should implement the purposes of the court's composition. The defendant should be found guilty only if the most qualified person so votes and it can fairly be concluded that any dissenting votes are idiosyncratic. We might then provide that a verdict of guilty requires the concurrence of at least eight members of the court among whom are the presiding judge and at least one of the two lawyers. One might require the vote of both lawyers to convict; or one might simply require unanimity of the whole court. While those higher requirements would presumably reduce the total number of convictions, they do

*In French courts, a member of the bar present in court may be called to sit on the panel of judges if one of the regular judges is unable to sit and no substitute judge is available. A variety of collateral benefits might result, among them that the large majority of lawyers who do not practice in criminal cases would become aware of and pay attention to the administration of criminal justice.

not add generally to the qualifications of the court and are unlikely to increase the capacity of the proceeding to avoid a wrongful conviction. The same degree of unanimity should not be necessary for a verdict of not guilty. If a majority of the court including the judge or seven members of the court not including him voted to acquit, that verdict should be accepted.

The selection of two members of the bar and seven lay jurors should be accomplished administratively before the proceeding begins. The professional qualifications of lawyers should be sufficient to overcome anything except challenges for cause based on matters readily determined in advance. The general qualifications and disqualifications of lay jurors should similarly be determined administratively. Then, without a *voir dire* except in extraordinary cases (in which the presiding judge would inquire about and rule upon bases for excuse), the defendant should be allowed summarily to require replacement of as many of the original court, except the presiding judge, as he liked; and that is all. The state should have no replacements.

There is no way to show that a ten-member court so constituted would be superior to all the other combinations one might imagine. The size and composition of the court might be made to vary according to the seriousness and complexity of the case. While the selection of any precise formula in comparison with other closely similar ones is somewhat arbitrary, we can state the principles of selection and, so far as our experience permits, apply them. Manifestly, we do not do that now. A court composed along the lines suggested would be far more consistent with our objectives than the present jury of twelve lay persons openly selected so far as the lawyers are able according to their inclinations one way or the other.

The conduct of the proceeding is suggested by the

criticisms of the trial in Chapter 5. To avoid the domination and control of the prosecutor and defense counsel, the presiding judge should be responsible for the presentation of evidence. In the same way that now the lawyers study their respective cases before trial, the judge should study the magistrate's file before the proceeding begins. At the outset, he should outline the case against the defendant and the evidence for and against his guilt. The defendant should then be allowed to make a statement of his own, whether to outline the evidence himself or offer an explanation or simply to assert himself within the limits of decorum. Witnesses who were examined by the magistrate should then testify unless excused by prior stipulation of the defendant. The order in which witnesses testify should be determined by the judge, who should also indicate to witnesses the desired subjects and scope of their testimony. They should be asked to testify directly about the crime, questions being used to elicit the information and guide a witness toward what is relevant. The defendant should be included among the list of potential witnesses but decide himself whether he will testify or not. The members of the court should ask questions freely to resolve inconsistencies and ambiguities or to review points that they want clarified. The defendant also should be allowed to question a witness and to challenge or contradict him. When it may be helpful to resolve an issue, witnesses should confront one another. The role of the prosecutor and defense counsel during the presentation of witnesses should be that of advisers to the court. They should be allowed to recommend that witnesses be heard in a particular order or additional witnesses be heard, to recommend questions, and to suggest lines of inquiry to ensure that favorable evidence is not overlooked.

After all the witnesses have been heard, the defendant

should have another opportunity to address the court as he chooses. The prosecutor and defense counsel should also address the court to summarize the evidence and make any additional argument or plea. Following further discussion of the applicable legal principles as that is necessary, the court would withdraw to reach a verdict. Preceded by the magistrate's investigation and unencumbered by the tactics and delays of our adversary system, there would be few proceedings that were not concluded within a day.*

A proceeding conducted along these lines would be entirely unlike an American trial, although not so unlike proceedings in other countries. The departures from our existing practices are only the result of eliminating the adversary structure where its effect is not to further the goal of a prompt, accurate determination of guilt. In place of two "cases" each elaborately contrived to distort the whole, the evidence developed by the magistrate and preserved in his file would be submitted to the scrutiny and judgment of the court. At the same time, where partisan advocacy would assist the goals of the proceeding it would be retained. There is no reason why the defense counsel or prosecutor, having in mind the objective of the proceeding, should not recommend a course of action. More important, they should be present to watch out for and prevent inadvertent or deliberate bias in the presentation of the evidence. Arguments from both sides, like the closing arguments now, about how the court should view the evidence are likely to assist the court's deliberations. If the shift of the line between neutrality and advocacy seems strange in the context of a criminal trial, it is a far more normal one in our experience generally. But for

---

*Were our sentencing provisions reformed—reduced and standardized—the court should pronounce sentence at the same time that it declared a verdict of guilty.

its unfamiliarity, it is likely to be more easily understood, applied, and accepted than the line we draw now.

There is no way to demonstrate in advance that a criminal process shaped according to this outline would "work." A comparison of our process with those of some countries which follow a model closer to what I have outlined does not suggest that abstractly our process is superior. Aside from that comparison, which will not be helpful to persons unfamiliar concretely with the workings of another process, how does one respond to the predictable dismissal, "It wouldn't work"?

No one who took careful account of the purposes for which we have a system of criminal justice at all and the values we want to protect would set up the process we actually have. Were someone to propose it as a model for a society unfamiliar with it but claiming the same purposes and values as ours, surely the response would be incredulity, not only because "it wouldn't work" but because even if it could be made to "work" it would be so far from what was intended. Criminal justice is not a very high social priority, and we allow to persist a criminal process that is manifestly inefficient and unjust. But for their familiarity, our existing practices would appear to be much more far-fetched than what I have proposed.

The model outlined in this chapter is not derived from new principles. It is rather a straightforward application of principles that we already preach but do not practice. For the most part, it requires no new theoretical underpinnings, but only a willingness to depart from existing institutional arrangements and consider what alternative institutions would be most likely to make the principles effective. The establishment of an investigating magistracy would modify our present understanding of the separation of executive and judicial powers in the criminal process. But however strictly that principle is conceived as an abstract matter, in practice the police exercise "judicial" authority to require submission to arrest and investigation, and the prosecutor, as well as the defense counsel, exercises "judicial" authority to determine what the judgment of conviction will be. Those are not departures from the established process but what it prescribes. As for what would replace it, the application of judicial attributes to criminal investigation, so far as that can be achieved, is obviously desirable. Nor would the magistrate's determination of guilt, made promptly after the crime and embodied in a permanent record of his investigation, detract from the final judgment; we should have far more certainty of guilt than we have now from a negotiated plea or a trial dominated by adversary tactics long after the crime.

Judicial officials would have more responsibility for the final judgment, and lawyers less. That is not to be regretted, if the consequence would be a more, and more visibly, just process. The qualifications for the magistracy would require specialized preparation different from that of a police officer or a lawyer. The magistracy would have to be, as it is in many countries, a legal career for which one studied as one studies for legal practice. The prosecutor's office would perform different, narrower functions. The criminal-defense bar would be transformed. Defense lawyers would be obliged to meet the demands of a strict schedule and have a more substantial, more structured, and less isolated role in the criminal process, which would require skills different from those mainly required now. The private practice of criminal law would probably depart more sharply than it does now from most kinds of noncriminal legal practice. Lawyers whose practice consists mainly of criminal cases are already a small, distinct group within the profession; and there have been strong proposals to improve the practice of criminal law by limiting it to lawyers who have prepared themselves especially for it.

Large institutional changes of this kind are not easily accomplished and would understandably be resisted by the persons affected most directly. We should have to experiment repeatedly with measures the precise consequences of which could not be predicted in advance. Many individuals would face professional and personal dislocations that might benefit others more than themselves. However, the professional identities of the two groups most affected, the police and the criminal-defense bar, would be clarified and rationalized without loss of dignity to either. We cannot foresee that in the long run it will be any less difficult to keep what we have, which openly defeats both our ideals and our concrete social objectives.

The criminal process does not fail because the persons who carry it out are less responsible, learned, or just than they should be. Policemen and lawyers and others fill their roles competently and conscientiously within the existing institutional structure. Without expecting that new institutions will make new and better men, we can nonetheless create institutions that will bring official and professional conduct and its outcome closer to what we want. If social institutions do not immediately and automatically fulfill the objectives for which we intend them, neither are they intractably indifferent to our objectives. The criminal process as it is now is also the product of human invention. Unsuccessful as it is, the case for changing it is overwhelming.

Appendix

QUESTIONING THE DEFENDANT: THE DEFENDANT AS WITNESS

The extent to which investigative and prosecutorial procedures rely on "self-incrimination" is commonly regarded as a hallmark of two distinct kinds of process, the "accusatorial" and the "inquisitorial." In this country, a privilege against compulsory self-incrimination is constitutionally protected;[1] the privilege has been interpreted broadly as a right not to give evidence against oneself, which the government must assiduously protect. In other countries no less civilized, a person who is accused of a crime is expected to play a large role in the criminal process; his right *to give* testimony promptly and fully is emphasized and protected. Few issues in criminal process have been debated here as persistently and intensely— or resolved less satisfactorily. As police behavior, the practice of arresting a man in order to ask him what he knows about a crime that he probably committed is easily explained. As the all but exclusive means of questioning a suspect, it is a theoretically empty and curiously ambiguous resolution of the problem of

147

how and how far a person should participate in the development of proof of his own guilt.

Americans associate inquisitorial procedure with compulsion by torture to confess. There is remote and recent history to support the association. When criminal procedure crystallized on the European continent, torture to obtain a confession of guilt was an accepted practice. Oddly, the justification for torture was that a man could not be adjudged guilty if the proof were not certain, a theory that on its face was more solicitous of the accused than the less elegant approach of the emerging English procedure. It was understood that torture was allowed only if there was strong independent evidence of guilt; it could then be used as a last resort to obtain a confession that satisfied formal demands of the theory of proofs. But its use was not always so carefully restricted.[2] Although the inquisitorial model was not followed in the United States, use of the "third degree" on defendants in certain kinds of cases became common.

It has been easy for us to see the choice between a process that regards an accused person as a witness and one that regards him as privileged not to be a witness as a choice between compulsion or not, whether that view was thought to be conceptually accurate or simply validated by experience. So, for example, the Supreme Court made a dichotomy between a government which produces evidence against an accused without his aid and one which uses "the cruel, simple expedient of compelling it from his own mouth."[3] Yet, strongly as we have preferred an "accusatorial" process, no country relies so much as we on the defendant's formal acknowledgment of his guilt. Insistent that a defendant not be obliged to contribute to the evidence against him, nonetheless we readily accept his formal, ritualistic plea of guilty as sufficient basis to condemn and punish him. The issue of the defendant as witness has been all but buried under rhetoric which either proclaims that his freedom from participation in the investigation in any form is an "essential mainstay" of "the American system of criminal prosecution"[4] or declares that by giving him such freedom law enforcement irremediably cripples itself. Unsurprisingly, the rhetorical volume goes up when the ambiguity and inconsistency of our practices become most evident.

Sometime during the investigation of a crime or what may have been a crime the investigators are likely to want to talk to a person who is a suspect, unless the other evidence is unequivocal. It would be outrageous (and unconstitutional) to convict someone without letting him give his account of the event. No investigation which purposely excluded his account could be taken seriously. Nonetheless, our criminal process has moved very close to a model which so separates a suspect from the investigation of a crime that his account is heard, if at all, only after the investigation is complete. It is not far from the prevailing view that *because* we suspect someone we should not try to learn anything from him. Part of the explanation for such a peculiar position is that criminal process is conceived conclusively as a process against someone, between whom and the officials engaged in it, therefore, there is little communication. The concrete situations out of which that conception developed were ones in which the manifest need was not to encourage a suspect's participation in an investigation, but to separate him from it in order to protect him from abuse. The question whether it would be desirable for a suspect to participate as both a giver and receiver of information and, more particularly, to admit his crime if he is in fact guilty has had to be answered in the shadow of the third degree.

In the first cases in which the Supreme Court reversed a

conviction because the defendant's own statements were used against him, it was clear that the confession had been extracted by the worst methods. In one of the earliest cases, decided in 1936, one defendant was "hanged . . . by a rope to the limb of a tree," and then "tied to a tree and whipped"; later he was whipped again and told that the whipping would continue until he confessed. The other two defendants were taken to a jail where they "were laid over chairs and their backs were cut to pieces with a leather strap"; they too were told that the whipping would continue until they confessed. All three confessed. A few days later they were tried, convicted on the basis of the confessions, and sentenced to death.[5] Other cases as well confirmed the conclusion of the National Commission on Law Observance and Enforcement (the Wickersham Commission) in 1931 that use of the third degree was widespread.[6] The Commission's report described a variety of physical and psychological techniques designed to extract a confession against a person's will, which the cases illustrated.

Over the years the methods that the police used became more subtle and the justification for excluding a confession less certain. But the general principle was clear enough: A person must not be made to incriminate himself by the deliberate imposition of choices among which confession seemed the lesser evil or by the deliberate wearing away of a firmly made decision not to confess. There was a turning point in 1964 in the famous *Escobedo* case, which *Time* described as a "constitutional thunderbolt" and "cop's nightmare."[7] There, a majority of the Supreme Court revealed a scarcely concealed preference that a defendant not give any incriminating information to the police, at least in response to questioning by them. Two years later in another famous case, Miranda v. Arizona,[8] the Court announced rules which, if the police took them as seriously as they were apparently intended, would have made most police questioning ineffective.

Although the techniques of questioning had changed, it was as true in 1966 as it had been thirty years earlier that the purpose of questioning was to "get" a suspect to talk. All of the techniques that the police used and the Supreme Court finally rejected shared the assumption that, guilty or not, a suspect is well advised not to talk to the police. When the questioners tried to overcome his unwillingness to talk, it was not because they believed he had decided unwisely; on the contrary, they believed that he had made the wise decision, which happened, however, not to be the one they wanted him to make. There could be no honest effort, therefore, to convince him to change his mind. In place of the Wickersham Commission's report, the Supreme Court in *Miranda* had before it "interrogation manuals," guides to successful questioning, from which it quoted at length. The manuals are not discussions of the wisdom or social utility of confessing one's crime; they contain directions to tell a suspect that it would be wise and socially useful for him to confess, which is a different thing. From the point of view of the questioner, the suspect is merely a potential source of evidence which may be forthcoming by the application of proper techniques.

It did not occur to anyone to argue in *Miranda* or earlier that the state could properly and openly question a suspect because he *ought to* respond to its questions—that he had a legal or social or moral obligation to do so. The suspect's own proper position was simply irrelevant. Questioning was carried out at a different level, as a straightforward confrontation between his will and the state's power. Moreover, it was unregulated. When they questioned, the police were performing their general duty to investigate crime; but insofar as they were sequestering a particular individual, they were acting beyond their authority. Usually, the time for questioning was found by disregarding a requirement of prompt presentment before a magistrate following an arrest. The practice which the Court had before it in *Miranda* as much as in the earlier cases was formally unauthorized, unregulated, and unpublic; it was not carried out by persons trained or expected to give due weight to the variety of social interests at stake. The interest in investigation, of course, was often large; the defendant in *Miranda* for example, was accused of rape and murder.

Notwithstanding the evident, often proclaimed interest in confessions and repeated complaints that the courts were ignorantly denying us a necessary investigative tool, there has been no substantial effort to develop and implement procedures for questioning by means which a state might be willing not just tacitly to permit but to avow. One can speculate about the explanation for such a failure. No doubt the constitutional prohibition against compelled self-incrimination has chilled efforts to develop any formal, regular procedure whereby a man might incriminate himself. A procedure which lacked the manipulative techniques which are the very essence of custodial interrogation may have been thought bound to fail. The path, if indeed there were any, between unconstitutionality and inutility must have looked exceedingly straight and narrow.

Nevertheless, the theory and methods of police questioning as it has been practiced in this country do not fully define the issue of self-incrimination. The Supreme Court was surely correct in *Miranda* that the government should not employ techniques to get a person to do something which it is neither his obligation nor in his interest to do; the relationship between the individual and the government in this country does not allow the government to require conduct just because it "wants" it. But that is not the end of the matter.

When the authority of government is used to require a person to act as he otherwise would not, we do not assert simply that it will be helpful somehow to have the conduct performed and therefore that one way or another we shall get him to perform it. We assert that it is proper that he act in that way. Not only is there a social need; given the social need, the individual ought to do that which we require of him. We may recognize that he does not believe that he ought to act as we require, and respect his belief. We are prepared to insist on the conduct and even impose a penalty for nonperformance because, his belief notwithstanding, we adhere to our own judgment.*

Before we can consider what methods of questioning a suspect are permissible, we need to face the issue that is always ignored: Can the government properly assert that a person who is suspected of a crime ought to give information about it? Suppose that the manager of a company finds a serious error in an account. The company employs a dozen bookkeepers, any one of whom might have prepared the account. The manager believes that he can find out who made the error by carefully studying penmanship and adding-machine tapes, noting the work done by each book-keeper during the previous week, and so forth. Should he follow that course, or should he walk into the bookkeeping department with the flawed account and ask, "Who made

---

*Imagine that the government were to say to a man drafted into the army, "On the whole you are correct that this war is immoral and unwise; and you are correct in refusing to take the substantial risk of being killed to help us win it. Nevertheless, we find it convenient that you should serve in the army and we shall see to it that you do." There is more serious objection to such an approach than that it is a bad way to recruit.

this mess?'' Or suppose that a mother of three small children finds the cookie jar empty and a trail of crumbs leading inconclusively out of the kitchen. Should she "investigate"—watch to see who doesn't eat his dinner—or should she ask who ate the cookies?

It is not only considerations of efficiency that tell us that the right course in these cases is to ask. The widely shared moral and social judgment is that we ought to take responsibility for our acts and should be given the opportunity to do so. It is better for a person to assume responsibility for the consequences of his conduct than for responsibility to be imposed. After all, it was in response to his father's question that George Washington—so we used to be taught—told his father that he had cut down the cherry tree. The story would have quite a different point if his father had simply presented young George with proof of the misdeed. Being careless about bookkeeping or invading a cookie jar is not criminal. The cases of the careless bookkeeper and the cookie monster do, however, show that there is no general principle against acknowledging one's wrongdoing. There is a general principle, but it points the other way. If it does not apply to the confession of crime, that is because of features special to that context.

The grim conditions of our prisons and the lack of an even minimally persuasive theory to explain our treatment of prisoners make it easy to argue that no one can have a duty to bring about his own conviction if to do so has the consequence of imprisonment. More narrowly, one might argue that even if punishment by imprisonment is not intrinsically impermissible, it would be so disproportionate to the crime in a particular case that the defendant has no duty to acknowledge his guilt and accept imprisonment as a consequence. At the other extreme, a systematic revolutionary who denies the state's authority altogether (whether or not on general anarchic principles) will conclude that the authority to punish is lacking whatever the crime and whatever the punishment.*

Any of those theories may be held by the defendant himself or an observer of the criminal process. If so, we may be obliged to respect a defendant's determination not to confess. But the position that the punishment which a defendant will suffer if he is convicted is impermissible and therefore does not count as a proper consequence of his conduct is not one that the system which imposes the punishment can take. If the punishment is impermissible, we ought not to impose it in any case; an impermissible punishment is not less so because we allow the defendant to resist it. So long as we believe that the punishment is a proper consequence of guilt and propose to impose it if the defendant is guilty, then consistently with that belief the nature of the punishment is not an argument against voluntary confession.

If the general obligation to act responsibly is not inapplicable to criminal conduct because of the nature of the consequence(s), it is inapplicable nevertheless, it has been argued, because of the nature of the criminal process. The effectiveness of our adversary system, it is said, depends on "challenge," "a constant, searching, and creative questioning of official decisions and assertions of authority at all stages of the process."[9] To insist on plain and adequate justification for a criminal conviction is not, however, to

---

*A duty to confess may remain despite objection to the punishment, which is not always the most significant of the consequences. Even if one denies the validity of all the consequences, one may conclude that he has a duty to accept them. The nonrevolutionary, anyway, may conclude that he ought to submit to injustice rather than provoke disorder. Or one may perceive personal duties that require submission, as did Socrates in the *Crito* and, in another way, Sydney Carton in *A Tale of Two Cities.*

recommend hamstringing the investigation and prosecution of crime every time there is a chance. No one would argue that the sound administration of criminal justice requires that witnesses to a crime not report their testimony voluntarily to the police or that defendants and their lawyers delay trials for as long as they can get away with it. Effective challenge is not that indiscriminate. It is above all government policies as formulated and as applied that need to be challenged.

Acknowledging one's acts and accepting responsibility for them does not oblige one to accept without challenge a not inevitable consequence that he believes should not occur. It is not an evasion of responsibility to try to establish that a proposed punishment is not authorized or is bad social policy or is unjust. (Could anyone object if George Washington had tried to persuade his father not to take away his "little hatchet," so long as he did not deny that he had cut down the cherry tree?) Nor is it an evasion to contest the prosecutor's legal characterization of conduct and argue that it was a less serious crime than he asserts or was no crime at all. Challenges of this kind are different from and do not depend on a denial that one did what in fact one did.*

There may be a more general argument, that citizens ought to try to hamstring the government because by and large the government will succeed in desirable goals anyway and will become too strong unless opposed. That argument is plainly not intended to be taken literally. Even the most ardent advocate of small, weak government does not recommend automatic, indiscriminate opposition to a road project, a school lunch program, a criminal prosecution, compulsory

---

*Recognition of a duty to acknowledge one's actual conduct hardly creates any likelihood that factual disputes in the criminal process will become so rare that the factfinding process will be generally weakened by desuetude.

vaccination, automobile license requirements and everything else that a community may try to accomplish through its government. But if that is not what the argument means, it expresses only a political attitude or a political philosophy too general to resolve concrete issues. It does not make a case for denying one's own responsibility in the particular context of a criminal prosecution rather than any of the other possibilities for opposing the government.

There is a final argument that one ought not give information about his crimes: simply that it is never to the accused's advantage. His concern is only how to avoid punishment, and his course to that end is clear. To respond in that way to the state's claim to information is not to overcome the claim, but to ignore it. It is true, of course, that to tell a person what he ought to do is not to tell him what will profit him or what he will enjoy doing; indeed, the practice of telling a man that he will "feel better" if he confesses is one of the tactics that usually counts as manipulation. But that is not to the point.

These are, I think, the arguments against the proposition that a man who has committed a crime ought to acknowledge what he has done. The conclusion that follows from their rejection is perhaps small. It is only that the state does not pursue an improper objective when it asks a person for information that may incriminate him. If we have confidence in our system of criminal justice, it is correct and consistent with our fundamental principles, which make a person independent and responsible, that he acknowledge his acts even when they are criminal. We can, then, reach the question of method: are there ways to ask a person who is suspected of a crime to talk about it, without violating our principles?

Nothing that has been said supports the manipulative techniques that characterize police questioning. Methods that "get" a person to act in some way despite his will to act otherwise do not affirm his capacity as a moral agent on which his responsibility depends; they deny it. A moral imperative is neither a command nor a statement about what will happen. That a person ought to do something does not entail even that he should be required to do it, much less that he should be made to do it. On the other hand, it may be appropriate to require performance of a social obligation, as we do in many other contexts. Or, if its performance should not be required, it may be appropriate and useful to point out the existence of the obligation without more.

If a requirement that persons answer questions about criminal conduct would serve a social purpose and is consistent with our general views about individual morality, why should we not impose it? The government regulates our lives in so many other ways as a condition of living in community, and in particular it requires us to supply information in other contexts when that will serve a social purpose. While the government does not have a general right to any information it wants, a requirement that we furnish information relevant to the accomplishment of a specified social purpose is rarely questioned or even much noticed. As a general matter, "giving information" is not regarded differently from other kinds of duty that individuals may be called on to perform for the good of the community. Why should we balk at using the power of government to obtain information about crime? If a person can be required to give any other information, why draw the line at incriminating information, which is a protection only for those who commit crimes and even for them only insofar as they intend to evade punishment which the society intends that they not evade? (As it is presently interpreted, the constitutional privilege against self-incrimination has no application if a person does not risk prosecution or punishment. It is on that basis that "immunity" statutes, which allow the government to compel a person to reveal that he has committed crimes so long as it does not use the revelations against him, are upheld.[10])

Whether to impose a requirement and how it shall be enforced are separate questions. The penalty for nonperformance need not be so great that it raises the specter of self-incrimination by the innocent or converts the requirement into "compulsion."* Even though it may deprive a confession of the moral quality of a free act, the objection to a requirement of self-incrimination is not that some persons would comply with it. The major objection is that predictably many, probably most, would not. Unlike most requirements that have a penalty for nonperformance, performance of a requirement of self-incrimination would itself subject one to a criminal penalty with which the penalty for nonperformance could be directly compared.

In the end, a requirement of self-incrimination should not be imposed because it will not be effective. If the penalty is small, it will be borne; and if it is large, it will be avoided by perjury. It is difficult to prove that a man has wilfully failed to respond truthfully to questions without resorting to extrinsic evidence showing the contrary of what he said. Proof that a man testified falsely sufficient to warrant his punishment for perjury is not easily obtained. It is likely to be the same proof that would be used to convict him of the original crime. And in any case, it is doubtful that we could tolerate many convictions for perjury without convictions for the underlying crimes.

The argument against requiring a person to give evi-

---

*The penalty for violation of the tax laws, for example, is substantial; nevertheless we speak of a requirement that we pay our taxes, not compulsion. One way to demonstrate that a requirement is not strictly compulsion is to show that it is frequently disobeyed.

dence that may incriminate him is not nearly so strong as the argument against coercing him to do so, which is based on considerations of principle of a different order. We do require disclosure of information in a great many contexts in which we should not consider using coercion or what is the equivalent, manipulating a person to obtain the information. If a persuasive case were made that requiring the defendant to give evidence would significantly aid criminal process without undue cost, but for the constitutional prohibition we should consider imposing the requirement.* I doubt that the case can be made.

There remains the possibility of persuasion. We have learned to be wary of "persuasion," which has often been a euphemism for something much more like manipulation or coercion. There is a difference. We can readily imagine Washington Sr. trying to persuade young George that he should tell the truth without trying to trick him into doing so or "make" him do so. A man may persuade his wife to see a particular movie without luring her unaware into the theater or threatening some dire consequence if she sits at home. It is not difficult to distinguish between paradigmatic manipulation or coercion and persuasion, although at the margins persuasion shades imperceptibly into manipulation, as it does in advertising, or coercion, as it does if there is too plain a promise of too large a benefit which will otherwise be withheld.†

Recognition of a person as a responsible moral agent

---

*It is clear that the Fifth Amendment, as it has consistently been construed, does not permit the government to require self-incrimination; so far as the constitutional text is concerned, the reference to compulsion includes any form of official requirement that alters the balance to favor confession.

†One can go through the motions of persuasion without believing what he says. That is, of course, exactly what interrogation manuals advise a questioner to do. But such a technique, based on deceit, counts as manipulation.

and member of the community supports an effort to point out his obligation and persuade him to meet it. One may (try to) refrain from giving advice about a matter because it is none of his business or because it is worthwhile to encourage independence of judgment. But a position of uninvolvement (represented by the formula "Do as you please") has no general preference. Whatever the extent of individual responsibility to other individuals, it may be argued, the *state* has no business trying to persuade; a state should require what it must require and otherwise leave its citizens alone. As a description of how this or any developed society operates, that proposition is certainly false. Our government promotes a vast range of social policies by methods of persuasion that do not involve requirements. Nor does the argument stated so generally make sense. Why should the government be limited to the grosser methods of getting the society's work done? The suggestion that by limiting the means one can limit the ends is doubtful; more likely one will affect the choice of means.

Whatever the propriety of persuasion in general, it may be argued that it simply is too much to ask of a person that he bring about his own condemnation and imprisonment. However, if condemnation and imprisonment are an appropriate consequence of his conduct, there is no reason why a representative of the state should not try to persuade him that that is so. Indeed, if the state regards him still as a member of the community, there is every reason why it should try to persuade him that it is so. It may be "too much to ask" in the sense that many persons will not accept such an obligation. But so long as no penalty follows from their failure, there is no harm in asking. The obligation that is involved is not only a matter of private morality; it is also the business of the state, which may properly claim an interest in its performance.

The most substantial argument against any official effort

to question a suspect is that given an opportunity to ask questions, few questioners will be able to stop at that; someone who is professionally interested in the result and who believes that the person he is questioning has committed a serious crime will encourage or cajole or insist or coerce. He will resort to manipulation of the person questioned. The end determines the means, and the end is to obtain an answer. Our experience of police questioning cautions against readily accepting any claim that a procedure for questioning is not coercive or manipulative. The techniques that the police have used were dictated mostly by the "need" for a confession rather than an independently derived, controlling set of restraints. Questioning practices have not been wholly intractable to rules, however. Between the earliest cases and *Miranda*, the standards for questioning changed, probably as much as the basic fact that the questioners were the police allowed. Our experience does not show that if the government through its officials asks any questions at all, there has been bullying; that makes too much of the government's power and too little of the distinction between having power and using it. We ought to put a heavy burden of proof on someone who purports to describe a procedure for asking questions that is neither coercive or manipulative nor dependent on a requirement to answer. But we need not assume in advance that the burden cannot be met.

Another way of stating the same objection is that no manner of questioning that does not depend on some form of coercion or manipulative technique will be effective; questions will not produce honest answers unless the self-interest of the person questioned is overcome. Our experience is otherwise. People expect to know their obligations and expect to perform them. We ordinarily rely for the performance of socially imposed obligations, even onerous ones, on an intricate fabric of rules, customs, institutions, habits, and individual and social pressures that contradict a wholly self-interested "economic" calculation of means and ends.* Within the criminal process even in its present form, which makes opposition rather than obligation critical, defendants respond to perceived expectations and accept the roles assigned to them. The intuition that criminals will not give evidence against themselves is based on an institutionally validated understanding that they should not do so, not on an ineluctable, socially undetermined human characteristic. Of course it is not the case that all we need to do to obtain evidence of crimes is ask the suspect for information. But if the criminal process contained a normal expectation that a person suspected of having committed a crime would respond to questions about it, our ordinary experience and common sense (as well as considerable theory of human behavior) suggest that often he would do so.

Properly conducted, questioning a suspect in a judicial atmosphere as part of a general investigation of the crime would serve the investigative purpose consistently with the privilege against self-incrimination. One could not conduct a complete investigation without at least giving a suspect an opportunity to participate and to make a statement if he wished. Explicit acceptance of questioning by a magistrate would for some people raise constitutional issues that the less formal or open practice of police questioning does not raise. Just the same, proper magisterial questioning would comply more closely with the constitutional values than what commonly occurs now in police stations.

Because the magistrate who questioned a defendant would himself be partly responsible for the judgment of conviction and his file would be available to the court, we could not maintain the premise, as we do now, that no

---

*The argument above that a requirement would seldom be effective does not mean that a requirement is always necessary, but that if it were necessary it would seldom be sufficient.

implication of guilt is drawn from a defendant's refusal to give any evidence. That premise is embodied in a constitutional rule prohibiting the prosecutor and judge from commenting adversely to the jury about the defendant's silence. Most people assume, however, that jurors who see the defendant silently in court while all the witnesses talk about his conduct make the implication for themselves; many defense lawyers feel compelled to call the defendant to testify unless there are the strongest reasons to the contrary. Magisterial questioning would increase that kind of pressure on a defendant not to remain silent, even if lay jurors were carefully instructed that he was not required to speak and—if it were thought to have value—the prosecutor were prohibited from mentioning the defendant's silence in his closing argument. So far as the magisterial proceeding itself is concerned, the "no-comment rule" would have no application. Such a solution to the problem of implication from a defendant's silence would be far more comprehensible than our present, ostrich-like formula. The defense lawyer would be able to explain to the defendant more concretely and without technicality what the consequence of his silence was likely to be.

Freed from the constraints imposed by police investigation and an adversary trial as they are now conducted, the rules protecting the privilege against self-incrimination would undoubtedly be somewhat different from what they are. The rules that would be modified, however, protect the appearance of the privilege more than its substance. So long as the right to remain silent is respected and is neither concealed nor undermined by tactics deliberately designed to overcome it, it does no violence to the values of the privilege if a person who is believed to have committed a crime is asked questions as part of the state's effort to obtain a full, accurate determination of guilt.

NOTES

NaNCHAPTER 1

1. See page 78 and note 2.
2. The provisions of the Bill of Rights which affect criminal process are:

The Fourth Amendment: The right of the people to be secure in their persons, houses, papers, and effects, against unreasonable searches and seizures, shall not be violated, and no Warrants shall issue, but upon probable cause, supported by Oath or affirmation, and particularly describing the place to be searched, and the persons or things to be seized.

The Fifth Amendment: No person shall be held to answer for a capital, or otherwise infamous crime, unless on a presentment or indictment of a Grand Jury, except in cases arising in the land or naval forces, or in the Militia, when in actual service in time of War or public danger; nor shall any person be subject for the same offense to be twice put in jeopardy of life or limb; nor shall be compelled in any criminal case to be a witness against himself, nor be deprived of life, liberty, or property, without due process of law. . . .

The Sixth Amendment: In all criminal prosecutions, the accused shall enjoy the right to a speedy and public trial, by an impartial jury of the State and district wherein the crime shall have been committed, which district shall have been previously ascertained by law, and to be informed of the nature and cause of the accusation; to be confronted with the witnesses against him; to have compulsory process for obtaining witnesses in his favor, and to have the Assistance of Counsel for his defence.

The Eighth Amendment: Excessive bail shall not be required, nor excessive fines imposed, nor cruel and unusual punishments inflicted.

The requirement of indictment by a grand jury has been applied only to federal prosecutions. All of the other provisions apply to both federal and state criminal cases, although not always with the same significance for both.

3. For examples of the shift, compare Miranda v. Arizona, 384 U.S. 436 (1966), with Harris v. New York, 401 U.S. 222 (1971); or United States v. Wade, 388 U.S. 218 (1967), with Kirby v. Illinois, 406 U.S. 682 (1972).

4. The statutes are 18 U.S.C. § 3501 (overruling the decision in *Miranda,* note 3 above, about police interrogation) and 18 U.S.C § 3502 (overruling the decision in *Wade,* note 3 above, about lineups). The Supreme Court seems to have concluded that Congress does not have that authority, since even the justices who do not like the rulings in question do not use the statutes to limit them; but it has never said so.

5. Gideon v. Wainwright, 372 U.S. 335, 344 (1963).

6. Argersinger v. Hamlin, 407 U.S. 25 (1972). On at least two occasions in the preceding nine years, some justices called attention to (and dissented from) the Court's refusal to consider whether the right to counsel applied to prosecutions for misdemeanors. Winters v. Beck, 385 U.S. 907 (1966); DeJoseph v. Connecticut, 385 U.S. 982 (1966).

CHAPTER 2

1. For a particularly vivid example of analytic detail that is functionally meaningless, see the line of cases discussing the meaning of "probable cause" for an arrest or a search, including among others Aguilar v. Texas, 378 U.S. 108 (1964); Spinelli v. United States, 393 U.S. 410 (1969); and United States v. Harris, 403 U.S. 573 (1971).

2. For example, at the end of an opinion restricting police questioning which *Time* (April 29, 1966, at p. 52)

called a "cop's nightmare" and which prompted the strong-est reaction in police circles, the Supreme Court calmly observed: "Nothing we have said today affects the powers of the police to investigate 'an unsolved crime,' . . . by gath-ering information from witnesses and by other 'proper investigative efforts.'" Escobedo v. Illinois, 378 U.S. 478, 492 (1964). Similar assurances are common in the Court's opinions.

    3. Draper v. United States, 358 U.S. 307, 313 (1959), quoting Carroll v. United States, 267 U.S. 132, 162 (1925).

    4. Pendergrast v. United States, 416 F.2d 776 (D.C. Cir. 1969).

    5. Rios v. United States, 364 U.S. 253, 256 (1960).

    6. "An absolute essential in the building of a good police force is the matter of reports. No modern business concern would dream of carrying on for even a day without having a complete system of recording its work; and yet few police forces in this country keep records that would even remotely compare with those of the average business house. It would seem, as the first principle in efficiency, that the head of every police force should have laid before him daily a summary of crime conditions in the city, and that at the end of the year he should make a complete public report, not merely of the arrests but of the complaints as well. . . . The lack of adequate statistical information bearing on the activi-ties of the police in the suppression of crime is certainly one good explanation of the prevalence of crime in American cities." National Crime Commission, "Criminal Statistics and Identification of Criminals," a report submitted to the National Crime Commission by the Sub-committee on Pardons, Parole, Probation, Penal Laws and Institutional Correction (1927).

    "Eventually a psychiatrist and social worker may be found in every police station. Until such case study under experts can be undertaken, the arrest record must continue to be a simple summary of very obvious physical and social data, which ordinary patrolmen can secure with a minimum of effort. Here we can find the prisoner's sex, age, race, education, social condition, employment, etc. These data are valuable when taken in the mass and when studied. For example, in Detroit we are just concluding an examination of 200,000 arrests. As a result we shall know something about the amount and character of offenses committed by different races, the ages at which offenders commit these offenses, the effect of domestic conditions upon the commission of offenses, as well as the part played by an absence of familiarity with a skilled trade." Lent B. Upson, "Crime Statistics as a Police Problem," *Proceedings of the American Statistical Association,* March 1928.

7. The Supreme Court has ruled in effect that an arrested person may be searched at the police station or jail for no other reason than that he has been arrested, so long as he is not subjected to harassment or abuse. The "essence" of such situations, it said, was that the "legal arrest of a person . . . does—for at least a reasonable time and to a reasonable extent—take his own privacy out of the realm of protection from police interest in weapons, means of escape, and evidence." United States v. Edwards, 415 U.S. 800, 808–09 (1974), quoting from United States v. DeLeo, 422 F.2d 487, 493 (1st Cir. 1970).

Questioning at the police station is subject to rules which at least formally restrict it considerably. The main case is Miranda v. Arizona, 384 U.S. 436 (1966).

8. United States v. Wade, 388 U.S. 218 (1967); Schmerber v. California, 384 U.S. 757 (1966).

9. See, for example, the statement of the Supreme Court in United States V. Edwards, note 7 above.

10. Miranda v. Arizona, note 7 above. The constitutional justification for the requirements, the Court said, was the privilege against self-incrimination.

11. United States v. Wade, 388 U.S. 218 (1967). The Court relied on the Sixth Amendment's guarantee of the right to counsel. That holding has since been limited to cases in which the police arrest someone after formal proceedings have been initiated in some way, for example by filing of a complaint or return of an indictment. Kirby v. Illinois, 406 U.S. 682 (1972). The effect of that limitation is to make the previously announced rule inapplicable in the majority of ordinary cases, in which the police themselves begin pro-

ceedings against a person after they have arrested him and completed whatever investigative steps, including a lineup, they decided to take. See pages 54–55.

12. Johnson v. United States, 333 U.S. 10, 14 (1948).

CHAPTER 3

1. Miranda v. Arizona, 384 U.S. 436, 460 (1966), quoting from 8 Wigmore, Evidence 317 (McNaughton rev. 1961).

2. An appeal in the case is reported in United States v. McCoy, 475 F.2d 344 (D.C. Cir. 1973).

3. The Fifth Amendment requires that an accusation of "a capital, or otherwise infamous crime" be made by a grand jury. The quoted clause has been construed to mean generally felonies, crimes for which the authorized penalty is imprisonment for more than a year.

4. A proposal to add to the Federal Rules of Criminal Procedure a provision for reciprocal discovery of the names and addresses of opposing witnesses three days before trial was defeated in Congress in 1975. The report of the conference committee which deleted the provision said:

> A majority of the Conferees believe it is not in the interest of the effective administration of criminal justice to require that the government or the defendant be forced to reveal the names and addresses of its witnesses before trial. Discouragement of witnesses and improper contacts directed at influencing their testimony, were deemed paramount concerns in the formulation of this policy.

Conference report to accompany H.R. 6799, H.R. Report No. 94-414, 94th Cong. 1st Sess., July 28, 1975, at p. 12.

CHAPTER 4

1. Miranda v. Arizona, 384 U.S. 436, 460 (1966).

2. "An individual accused of crime may voluntarily, knowingly, and understandably consent to the imposition of

a prison sentence even if he is unwilling or unable to admit his participation in the acts constituting the crime." North Carolina v. Alford, 400 U.S. 25, 37 (1970). The New York Court of Appeals has upheld a defendant's conviction on a plea of guilty to a crime which was "logically and legally impossible." People v. Foster, 19 N.Y.2d 150, 152, 25 N.E.2d 200, 201 (1967). On April 4, 1973, the "Harlem Four," accused of murder in a famous case, pleaded guilty to manslaughter with the understanding that no sentence would be imposed; they immediately held a news conference outside the courtroom to proclaim their innocence. *The New York Times,* April 5, 1973, p. 1.

The separation between the defendant's plea of guilty and proof of his guilt is generally bridged, as in the Federal Rules of Criminal Procedure, by the ambiguous requirement that there be a "factual basis for the plea." Rule 11(f).

3. Brady v. United States, 397 U.S. 742 (1970); ABA Project on Standards for Criminal Justice, Pleas of Guilty 2 (Approved Draft, 1968).

4. Brady v. United States, note 3 above, at 753. The ABA Standards, note 3 above, provide that among the considerations which may justify a sentencing concession to a defendant who pleads guilty is that he "has acknowledged his guilt and shown a willingness to assume responsibility for his conduct." Standard 1.8(a) (ii).

5. ABA Standards, note 3 above, Standard 1.8(a) (i), (iii).

6. Brady v. United States, note 3 above, at 752.

7. United States v. Wiley, 267 F.2d 453 (7th Cir. 1959). See also United States v. Derrick, 519 F.2d 1 (6th Cir. 1975).

8. ABA Standards, note 3 above, Standard 1.8(b).

9. For a typical example of such schizophrenia, scarcely concealed, see Richard H. Kuh, "Plea Copping," 24 New York County Lawyers' Association Bar Bulletin 160, 165–166 (1967): "sentencing judges may legitimately consider *remorse* in meting out punishment. And while a guilty plea is strong evidence of such remorse, the defendant who goes to trial when the evidence against him is indisputable would seem in sorry shape to claim contrition, and to ask for any

consideration premised on that claim, when he appears for sentencing. I do not mean to suggest that defendants received *added* punishment for going to trial. That would be improper. But the *bona fides* of claimed remorse might require careful inspection when its earliest evidence appears after a trial in which the evidence was so incontrovertible as to render the proceeding little more than an inquest. A defendant's knowledge that in the absence of any truly triable issue, his guilty plea would gain him consideration on sentence would—at least to some extent—curb purposeless trials." Mr. Kuh had had long experience as a prosecutor when he made this statement. Several years later, he became District Attorney of New York County (Manhattan), one of the largest and most prestigious prosecutor's offices in the country.

CHAPTER 5

1. F. Lee Bailey and Henry B. Rothblatt, Fundamentals of Criminal Advocacy 285–86 (1974).

2. George W. Shadoan, ed., Law and Tactics in Federal Criminal Cases 265 (1964).

3. Johns v. Smyth, 176 F. Supp. 949 (E.D. Va. 1959).

4. See Monroe H. Freedman, "Professional Responsibility of the Criminal Defense Lawyer: The Three Hardest Questions," 64 Michigan Law Review 1469 (1966). See also Monroe H. Freedman, Lawyers' Ethics in an Adversary System viii (1975), where Mr. Freedman discusses the affair. He is currently dean of the Hofstra University Law School.

CHAPTER 6

1. The constitutional guarantee of the right to a jury trial does not require that a jury be composed of twelve persons. Williams v. Florida, 399 U.S. 78 (1970). As it is presently interpreted, it requires that a verdict of guilty be unanimous in federal criminal trials but not in state criminal

trials. Johnson v. Louisiana, 406 U.S. 356 (1972); Apodaca v. Oregon, 406 U.S. 404 (1972). Although there has been no decision to that effect, almost certainly a jury must be composed exclusively of lay jurors. The proposal for a mixed jury would require a constitutional amendment. Were the criminal process altered as I have proposed, so far as the states at least were concerned, the right to a jury trial as at present might be deemed inapplicable. See Duncan v. Louisiana, 391 U.S. 145, 149 n. 14 (1968).

APPENDIX

1. The Fifth Amendment provides: "[N]or shall [any person] be compelled in any criminal case to be a witness against himself. . . ."

2. See generally John H. Langbein, Torture and the Law of Proof: Europe and England in the Ancien Régime (Chicago: University of Chicago Press, 1977).

3. Miranda v. Arizona, 384 U.S. 436, 460 (1966).

4. Malloy v. Hogan, 378 U.S. 1, 7 (1964).

5. Brown v. Mississippi, 297 U.S. 278, 281–82 (1936).

6. Report on Lawlessness in Law Enforcement.

7. Escobedo v. Illinois, 378 U.S. 478 (1964). *Time,* April 29, 1964, p.52.

8. 384 U.S. 436 (1966).

9. Report of the Attorney General's Committee on Poverty and the Administration of Federal Criminal Justice (Allen Report) 11 (1963).

10. See, for example, Kastigar v. United States, 406 U.S. 441 (1972).

INDEX

173

DATE DUE

FEB 25 1980

JAN 25 1982

APR 26 1982

MAY 24 1982

JUL 12 1982

JUL 28 '91

SEP 08 '9

GAYLORD

PRINTED IN U.S.A.